Plautus in Performance

PLAUTUS

IN PERFORMANCE

The Theatre of the Mind

NIALL W. SLATER

Princeton University Press ~ Princeton, New Jersey

Published by Princeton University Press, 41 William Street,
Princeton, New Jersey 08540
In the United Kingdom: Princeton University Press,
Guildford, Surrey

ISBN 0-691-06624-8

Publication of this book has been aided by a grant from the
National Endowment for the Humanities

This book has been composed in Linotron Caslon

Clothbound editions of Princeton University Press books are
printed on acid-free paper, and binding materials are
chosen for strength and durability. Paperbacks, although
satisfactory for personal collections, are not usually
suitable for library rebinding

Printed in the United States of America by Princeton
University Press, Princeton, New Jersey

Library of Congress Cataloging in Publication Data

Slater, Niall W., 1954-
Plautus in performance.

Bibliography: p.
Includes indexes.
1. Plautus, Titus Maccius—Criticism and interpretation.
2. Plautus, Titus Maccius—Dramatic production. I. Title.

PA6585.S55 1985   872'.01   84-15958
ISBN 0-691-06624-8

Optimis Parentibus

CONTENTS

Titus Maccius Plautus, the flat-footed clown from Umbria, has been my companion and delight for more than a decade. I was first led to read him by a work of criticism, Erich Segal's excellent *Roman Laughter*. I am not quite sure why a public library in a small Ohio town purchased such a recondite volume, but I am immensely grateful, for Segal's work led me to explore and re-explore these plays in college and in graduate school. My own chief hope in writing this book is that I may entice yet others to discover Plautus' diversions and delights.

To this end I have attempted to address this book both to specialists in Roman literature and those interested in the history of drama in general. All extensive quotations from the plays have been translated, and I have preferred to err on the side of colloquialism, since the Latin of the originals is eminently, even joyously, speakable. Isolated words within the text have not been translated by and large. Such citations of individual words and lines are usually there to bolster a philological point, but I hope the broad lines of the argument will remain clear to the general reader.

My debts of thanks for help and inspiration are many, of which I can record only a few here. My chief thanks go to J. Arthur Hanson. Little of what I first wrote for his seminar six years ago remains in the present work, but the questions I pursued then with his encouragement are still at the center of my interest in Plautus. His instincts as an advisor have proved unerring, now restraining my wilder flights of fancy, now encouraging me to pursue a line of thought further. Michael Goldman cheerfully worked through Plautus' archaic Latin in order to provide me with his invaluable perspective as a specialist in postclassical drama. Froma Zeitlin, through her invigorating criticism of an earlier stage of this work, did much to shape my thinking about theatre and metatheatre. John Wright offered me both much-needed encouragement and searching criticism. George Ryan offered invaluable help in preparing the final stage of my manuscript. James Tatum, whose own splendid translations have just appeared as *Plautus: The Darker Comedies* (Johns Hopkins, 1983), lent his keen critical eye and ear to both my text and translations. Whatever poor things remain in either are, alas, mine own.

I am also most grateful to those who have supported various stages of this work. I began this study while James Rignall Wheeler Fellow at the American School of Classical Studies at Athens and pursued it while a Charlotte E. Procter Fellow at Princeton University. The National Endowment for the Humanities awarded me a summer research stipend, on which I revised and expanded the dissertation version. Finally, the University of Southern California provided a grant for the final preparation of the manuscript.

Athens – Princeton – Los Angeles
February 1980 – November 1983

Plautus in Performance

There is a place for discussion, for research, for the study of history and documents as there is a place for roaring and howling and rolling on the floor.
—Peter Brook, *The Empty Space*

CHAPTER I

Introduction: The Performance Dimension

The inadequate operation of reading a play this way [i.e., as self-contained literary artifact] has shamefully limited our understanding of major dramatic fields like those of the Greek Old Comedy, Plautus and his street plays, medieval cycles, the Commedia dell' arte, *the Restoration comedy, and the Victorian domestic drama. . . .*[1]
—*J. L. Styan*

NOTHING is more elusive than the theatrical moment. It exists only in the fleeting conjunction of players, audience, and play, for without any one element of this triad the resultant experience is simply not theatre. It is perpetually new, for audience, players, and even play change with each performance. It is rather like phlogiston in eighteenth-century theories of combustion: invisible, not to be identified with any other component, and yet essential for the spark to catch and become flame.

Nothing therefore seems more hopeless than the attempt to criticize this amorphous assembly of perpetual change we call theatre. If, as someone improving on Heraclitus suggested, you cannot even step into the same river *once*, how are we to interpret and criticize our experience of theatre?

An obvious way to deal with poetic drama is to treat it like lyric or epic: analyze the meters, the diction, the imagery. The exponents of New Criticism and similar approaches have provided and continue to provide valuable insights into tragic texts with such methods, and even some of Aristophanes' comedies have yielded surprising results to the searching critic. The comedies of Plautus, though, have in large part resisted such readings,[2] and have con-

---

[1] Styan (1975), 108.
[2] There have been notable exceptions, such as Leach (1969).

sequently stood much lower in critical estimation than more inter-
pretable plays.

Now, though, such literary readings of ancient drama have
begun to seem incomplete. The works of Oliver Taplin and Sander
Goldberg among others[3] have begun to recover for us the root sense
of the word *drama* as something *done*, enacted, performed, every
bit as much as something said or sung. The performance is as
important as the poetry.

In the following pages I have two purposes. The first of these
is nothing more complex than an attempt to demonstrate the value
of reading some representative Plautine comedies as performances.
Several of the plays considered here have not been critical favorites
in the past. I believe that an understanding of the dynamics of
performance will reveal the comic appeal of these plays more clearly
than poetic readings have done (and certainly more clearly than
traditional analyst criticism of Plautus, which has been more interested in the plays he read than the ones he wrote). My second purpose
has dictated the choice of only six plays out of the corpus. While
performance criticism has much to say about all the plays, I have
chosen to concentrate on those plays in which a certain theatrical
self-consciousness is essential to the play's overall impact. I have
tried in the readings and in the summary discussions to adduce
parallels to other plays in the corpus, but my focus will remain on
these six plays.

Performance criticism is by no means theoretically complex; it
is not necessary to master any body of received texts on the subject
in order to find this approach useful. It begins with the simple
proposition that a play is not a text but rather a total artistic event
which exists only in a theatre during a performance. The actors and
the audience are as much participants in the creation of this artistic
event as is the author's text. Literary criticism can tell us a great
deal about this text, but to criticize the play we must look, quite
simply, at the whole play.

Performance criticism has its roots in a number of develop-
ments in which, not surprisingly, studies of Shakespearean and
modern drama have led the way. These studies have emphasized the
two nontextual or subtextual elements of the theatrical triad: the

[3] Taplin (1978) and Goldberg (1980).

4

performers and the audience. Though not strictly performance criticism, C. L. Barber's *Shakespeare's Festive Comedy* was a pioneering study in the societal and festal background of Shakespearean comic theatre. In Plautine studies, Barber's lead was followed by Erich Segal in his admirable book *Roman Laughter*. The festal background of comedy within a society, however, does not provide a complete explanation of the form and functioning of a comic play in the theatre. A play is not a festival or ritual; it is an autonomous artistic creation of a finite number of artists (playwrights and players) for a specific theatrical occasion.[4] As such, it has its own dynamic within the theatre. The way a play functions as a play within the theatre has been studied with particular success in recent years by J. L. Styan, whose work will be cited regularly in the following pages. I will not attempt a summary of his work here; the interested reader is invited to consult the original texts (see Bibliography). Styan has done much to illuminate the dynamics of interaction both among the performers and between stage and audience. He shows how elements as diverse as the architecture of the theatre and the expectations of the audience combine to produce theatrical meaning.

At first glance the need to reconstruct both performance and audience would seem to create an insuperable barrier to the performance criticism of Plautine drama.[5] Essentially nothing survives of Plautine theatre but the texts. There were no permanent stone theatres in Plautus' day in Rome, and no satisfactory visual record (in the form of vase paintings or other artistic representations) or verbal description of these temporary theatres survives.[6] We have little information on the costumes of the actors or, far more im-

---

[4] I will for the moment beg the question of the religious background of classical drama. Even though a Plautine play might have been commissioned for the *Ludi Apollinares*, that does not render the play a religious ritual.

[5] This point can be overemphasized or misunderstood. Strict archaeological reconstruction of vanished performances is *not* the goal of performance criticism. Nonetheless, plays conceived within widely differing conventions and playhouses (e.g., mediaeval mystery plays and Victorian melodrama) are as generically different as comedy and tragedy and must be read differently—even if we cannot fully recover the precise look of one type (e.g., the mystery play). Oliver Taplin in *Greek Tragedy in Action* (1978) has an illuminating chapter on this point in regard to tragedy (chap. 11, "Round Plays in Square Theatres"), which has a wider applicability.

[6] See Beare (1963), 176-83, for what can be guessed.

portant, on their masks.[7] We have no contemporary descriptions of performances that would tell us not only about staging, costumes, and masks, but also about acting styles, which are a vital component of theatrical meaning. In short, we have none of the information that has made possible the detailed study of Elizabethan and Jacobean theatre in recent years by performance critics like Styan.

Even worse, the texts themselves sometimes seem to be quicksand beneath our feet. As with all ancient literature, various corruptions have entered the texts as they have been passed down through manuscripts, posing problems some of which have not as yet admitted of solution. Typically in ancient theatre texts the manuscripts do not clearly indicate the speakers of lines, only changes of speaker, so that assignments of lines to speakers is often somewhat conjectural. Finally, as long as the scripts were still being played there remained the danger that actors or subsequent producers might interpolate their own additions or variations within Plautus' original text. Occasionally it is clear from the text that this has happened (see below on the prologue of the *Casina*). More often it is only a suspicion.[8]

Traditional philological criticism of Plautus has performed an invaluable service in laboring to remove such corruptions from the Plautine texts. We cannot, however, wait for the resolution of all textual disputes to universal satisfaction before beginning literary and performance criticism of the texts. Accordingly, it is useful, and indeed necessary to make the following assumption, even though it is patently untrue: we will consider Lindsay's Oxford text of a play to be the play script. Occasional points of dispute over readings or line attributions will be found in the notes, but these will not be our focus.

Another traditional problem of Plautine scholarship is also confined to the footnotes insofar as possible: the problem of the Greek original. Most if not all of Plautus' plays are based upon previous works of Greek New Comedy. Much nineteenth-century

---

[7] It is assumed in the following pages that actors in Plautine drama wore masks. See Beare (1963), 184-95 and 303-9. Gratwick (1982), 83-84, neatly summarizes the argument for masks. For a challenging recent statement of the opposite point of view, see della Corte (1975), 163-93.

[8] For a brief summary of the history of the texts, see Duckworth (1952), 437-41. For a more detailed treatment, see Pasquale (1952), 331-54.

scholarship, convinced of the superiority of Greek theatrical culture to that of Rome, mined the plays of Plautus for clues to the nature of the supposedly superior Greek text behind the Latin play. I hope that by now it is no longer necessary to argue the dubiety of the assumption of Greek theatrical superiority. If the recent fragments of Menander have proved nothing else, they have shown that the reputed master of New Comedy could, on occasion, be remarkably dull.[9] Finally, Plautus must be viewed as an artist in his own right. Whatever his sources, he, and he alone, is responsible for the shape of the Latin play he has created and for its artistic success or failure.

Once we have a text, we can extrapolate a good deal from it about performance. The basic facts of movement and the outline of the stage picture emerge easily from the texts; in movement and picture lies the bulk of the nonliterary meaning of a play. Repeated patterns of actor/audience interaction reveal themselves as conventions (e.g., the aside or the eavesdropping scene). Once identified as conventions, their functioning within a scene can be studied. By studying several plays, we can begin to see an entire network of convention and audience expectation against which meaningful variations can be played.

We have also begun to learn a good deal more about the third vital component of the theatrical triad, the audience. Segal has explicated the psychology of the Roman audience and the appeal of Plautus' plays to that audience in terms of Saturnalian revel and release. Recent research has also done much to dispel the notion that Plautus' audience were dolts quite ignorant of the nature and devices of theatre (the ancient equivalent of the apocryphal cowboys who shot up silent movie screens when the villain came on).[10] Theatre as a hellenized form was already a generation old, and his audience would have had contact with both native Italian forms of drama and the repertoire of the touring hellenistic acting companies.[11] Bruno

[9] He could also be remarkably skillful, as Goldberg (1980) has shown— but rarely funny.

[10] For a balanced assessment of Plautus' audience and its capabilities, see Handley (1975).

[11] See Gratwick (1982), 77-84, 96-97, for the influence of the repertoire of the Artists of Dionysos on Plautus' choice of Greek models for his plays. See also Wright (1982), 502, on the theatrical culture of his audience.

7

Gentili has demonstrated the existence in south Italy of a tradition of performing tragic excerpts, often from several diverse sources, in a form of anthological drama, and has suggested an influence of this practice on early Roman theatre.[12] His researches are sure to have significant impact on future discussions of Plautine sources, but for our purposes here his most significant finding is that Greek theatre was a living influence at Rome as a performing tradition, not merely in the form of literary texts, and that this performing tradition contrasted sharply with Roman theatre practice.

The nature of that Roman tradition is still something of a mystery. The most important factors seem to have been the Atellan farce and the mime. Our evidence for Atellan farce is late, from a literary stage of its development. The early Atellan farce was apparently an improvisational form with stock characters and simple plot scenarios, embellished with jokes and comic stage business *ad libitum* by the performers.[13] The analogy of commedia dell' arte is of course tempting and in broad outline quite useful as a picture of the Atellan performances. The most important feature of the analogy is improvisation. Each performance has a core of narrative that must be gotten through, but the performers are free—indeed expected— to improvise *lazzi* or humorous stage business and character turns. In fact, the audience comes for just this improvisation, for the plots of commedia and presumably the Atellan farce were banal in the extreme. Only the vitality of the moment, the sense of present creativity on the part of the performers, saves such drama from becoming stale and hackneyed.

In Plautus, the Greek, South Italian, and Roman theatrical traditions collide with explosively creative results. This is not the place for another disquisition on the impact of Greek literature on Rome through the cultural contact following the Punic Wars and the consequent beginnings of recorded Roman literature. Nor would another survey of the few facts and many conjectures about Plautus' biography be appropriate. We need merely note that Plautus had certainly worked in the Roman theatre before he turned to writing plays based on Greek models: he was a theatre professional to begin with.[14]

---

[12] Gentili (1979).
[13] Duckworth (1952), 11-17.
[14] I accept the belief of Duckworth (1952), 49-51, that Plautus was an actor,

As a professional he was in a far better position to note the differences in convention and dramatic functioning between Greek New Comedy and his native Italian traditions. Gentle Terence wrote beautiful Latin verse that captured the spirit of New Comedy—and failed repeatedly the crucial dramatic test of a theatre and an audience. Plautus made his living from the theatre, the first professionally self-supporting playwright in the history of world literature.[15] He knew theatre as a craft, not as a literary study, and his huge success in antiquity is testimony to how well he knew that craft.

In transforming Greek New Comedy by the process he describes as *vortere*, then, Plautus knew he had not merely to translate but to re-theatricalize an alien drama for his Roman audience. Plautus was unusually aware of theatre as theatre. He knew its artifices and commented on them for his own and his audience's amusement.

A mere reading of examples of Plautine drama using the methods of performance criticism would be a useful contribution to our understanding of the nature of Plautus' achievement, but I have chosen rather to concentrate the performance reading on the phenomenon of theatrical self-consciousness in Plautus. The most productive pathway into this study has proved to be the conventions of Plautine drama—as undoubtedly the Romans would find a study of the alien conventions of realism (the picture frame and the invisible fourth wall) the easiest pathway into modern drama.

First we need to clarify the term *convention*. In the field of ancient drama, David Bain has recently repeated the traditional definition of *convention* as audience acceptance of a technical device of the dramatist which is not realistic.[16] From an extremely narrow perspective (i.e., from that of the mid-nineteenth through twentieth centuries) this may seem an adequate definition. For most of the history of drama, however, including ancient drama, it seems dangerously misleading.

Bain's definition is tied to a traditional conception of theatrical illusion or "pretence," a term he would prefer. The convention then is seen as a substitute or short-hand for the illusion of reality that

---

presumably in Atellan farce or mime. He may even have acted in his own plays (see below on *Pseudolus*). The magisterial discussion of Plautus' life remains Leo (1912), 63-86.

[15] Segal (1968), 1-2.
[16] Bain (1977), 1-12.

9

would otherwise occupy its place. Traditional conceptions of the classical theatre have seen illusion or pretence as a chief aim of the artist. Aristotle's theory of mimesis has been decisive in shaping most Western theorizing about theatre. Fortunately, as in most other fields, theory has had little influence on popular theatrical practice.

Illusion is not the aim of all theatre. It certainly is the aim of late nineteenth- and early twentieth-century drama, and may have been the aim of Greek tragedy as well.[17] We have no necessary grounds for assuming, however, that it was the aim of Plautine comedy, not even if it can be argued that it was the aim of the Greek New Comedy works he was engaged in transforming.

J. L. Styan gives this succinct summary of the difference between illusory and non-illusory theatre:

> Illusion is the province of all theatre: a spectator goes to the playhouse in the expectation that he will be free to indulge it. In an introduction to Pirandello's *Six Characters in Search of an Author*, Lionel Trilling wrote, "The word *illusion* comes from the Latin word meaning 'to mock' (*illudere*), which in turn comes from the word meaning 'to play' (*ludere*), and a favourite activity of the theatre is to play with the idea of illusion itself, to mock the very thing it most tries to create—and the audience that accepts it." The term *illusion* is obviously an embarrassment for criticism, and has been for years. The theatre which pretends an illusion, whether of real life or of fantasy, is to be distinguished from that which simply makes the occasion for imaginative activity, some of which may be illusory. The basis of Ibsen's theatre is illusory, at its best making an audience believe in the images it creates on the stage, while the basis for Sophocles's theatre is non-illusory, never expecting belief in what is seen. The former mode is circumscribed by what is

---

[17] See Sifakis (1971), chap. 1, for further evidence of the lack of illusion in Greek comedy and some stimulating suggestions about illusion in tragedy. Bain (1977), 3-7, offers some useful criticisms of Sifakis. The Brechtian analogy Sifakis offers for lack of illusion in Old Comedy is perhaps misleading in that Brecht represented a reaction *against* illusion, whereas Old Comedy did not have a strongly illusory tradition behind it (like that of nineteenth-century drama) against which to react. Plautus, coming after the illusionism of New Comedy, was in a position to react against such a tradition.

> plausible; the latter has infinite flexibility and its drama can circle the globe, pass from the present to the past or the future, and leap from this earth to the clouds. The neutral stage allows an inexhaustible succession of dramatic images.[18]

I will argue that the Plautine stage, too, is a neutral stage, not bound by time, space, or realistic plausibility, a home to both illusory and non-illusory playing.

In what follows I will have occasion to use terms like *illusion*, *illusory*, and *illusionistic space*, for which I offer the following working definitions. An illusion exists in Plautus when two or more characters interact (by speech and behavior) according to audience expectations based on probability. These audience expectations include those based on knowledge of a character's stock type. An audience expects a *senex* to oppose his son's amours and accepts his doing so as a convincing illusion. *Illusionistic space* is a somewhat metaphorical term to describe the area over which audience expectations of probablity operate. In an eavesdropping scene, those being eavesdropped upon are within an illusionistic space. The eavesdropper(s) is (are) in a separate space, which may or may not be illusionistic itself.

A convention then is simply a highly structured means of dramatic communication, what Keir Elam has termed a "subcode" within the larger dramatic and theatrical codes which govern the whole performance.[19] The success of such conventions, whether of acting style or dramatic situation, is not to be measured by their approximation to reality but by their effectiveness as communication. As Bernard Beckerman has commented on the eavesdropping scene which will occupy a great deal of our attention in this work:

> Since Shakespeare introduced such [eavesdropping] scenes in more than half the plays he wrote, he must have found them an extremely useful means of enriching the dramatic appeal of

---

[18] Styan (1975), 180-81.

[19] Elam (1980), 52-53. Actually for such a modern critic Elam has rather narrow ideas about the goals of conventions. He suggests in his principal discussion of conventions (87-92) that even devices which break the frame of the action serve only to emphasize the facticity of representation, which seems to me to be utterly false.

his works. Such a device or convention, enables him . . . to select dramatic activity from artistic tradition, thereby gaining readily accepted dramatic tools. Whatever feedback occurred related not to life but to imaginative dramatic practice. Invention rather than credibility was the seal of authenticity. . . .[20]

So too we should not allow our modern expectations of the goals of the actor to prejudice our examination of Plautus' stock character conventions. Realism is simply another convention, whether in characterization or action.[21]

Several non-illusory conventions will concern us particularly in the analyses of plays that follow and should be defined here: the monologue, the aside, eavesdropping, role-playing, and the play-within-the-play. The monologue or soliloquy is any speech delivered by a character who is alone or believes himself to be alone on stage. It may be addressed to audience, self, or the gods. An eavesdropping scene occurs when one character (or more) is aware of the presence of another (or others) on stage, and the reverse is not true (i.e., those within the scene are unaware of the presence of eavesdroppers). Role-playing occurs whenever a character behaves in a manner not true to stock type. Play-within-the-play is a much looser term that I use for a scheme or trick which is controlled by a character of the outer play and behaves as a conventional play plot would.

This controlling character is the playwright of the play-within-the-play. The reader may object to this as mere metaphor. There are only three explicit mentions of characters as playwrights (literally poets, but clearly dramatic poets from contexts) in the corpus: *Asinaria* 748 and *Pseudolus* 401 and 404. In the other plays my justification for speaking of playwrights must be functional, not philological. The conception illumines the functioning of the plays as no other reading has.[22]

The playwright may work either through other actors alone or

---

[20] Beckerman (1979), 26.

[21] Styan (1975), 141: ". . . conviction of reality is only one, relatively minor, purpose the actor may pursue. Realism in characterization is so recent an objective for the actor that it does not seem unfair to see it as merely a period convention like any other. . . ."

[22] Lionel Abel offers a similar defense of the use of these concepts in his discussion of playwrights and plays-within-plays: Abel (1963), 49.

may himself participate in the play he is creating. In the former case he is a more literary playwright. He lays the course of the play out in advance by careful instructions to the players. He may also give further instructions in the course of the action. In the latter case he is a more improvisational playwright. Through his own acting he influences the acting of others. The course of the play is constantly subject to revision as in the course of playing revision is shown to be necessary.

Neither the literary (scripted) nor the improvisational playwright exists in a pure form in any of the following plays. In Plautus the two roles are merely two ends of a spectrum. Consequently, I will sometimes speak of the playwright or poet and sometimes of the improvisational lead player, but the role is in essence the same. Only the degree of previous preparation for the actions of the playwright (considerable in the case of the literary playwright, little or none for the improvisational) differentiates the two.

To speak of improvisation in a dramatic text, as I often will in these discussions, might seem as oxymoron. Improvised theatre per se cannot be scripted. It does, however, behave in certain recognizable ways. The hallmark of improvisation is a constant emphasis on action as presently happening and evolving: "now I will try this . . . ," "now I need a new scheme. . . ." Improvised theatre is paratactically structured, with little interweaving of action within a scene. Various actions, some abortive, some successful, follow and interrupt one another. One player may be generally in control of the others in an improvisation, but he cannot control completely the action of a scene. All these features of improvisation can be imitated in scripted theatre. Therefore, when I speak of improvisation, I mean Plautus' literary imitation of these features of improvisational theatre.

Finally, it is necessary to confront a term that will recur frequently in the following pages: *metatheatre*. As metalanguages to describe metafictions proliferate in the critical landscape, such a term needs more than a definition. It needs a defense.

Though doubtless some critic may have used the term before, recent discussions of metatheatre principally derive from Lionel Abel's seminal book, *Metatheatre*, published in 1963, in which he postulates that metatheatre is a form which came to replace tragedy sometime during the Renaissance and whose fundamental assumptions are that the world is a stage, life is a dream.[23] Metaplays, the individual representatives of metatheatre, are theatre pieces about life seen as already theatricalized.[24] One need not adopt Abel's belief that metatheatre has replaced tragedy as a genre to see that his general categorization of metaplays as a separate class can be a critically useful concept. Nor, even more importantly, need one see metatheatre as the dramatic expression of a culture's world-view: metatheatre is the autonomous creation of the theatre.[25]

Metatheatre has recently been defined as a quite different concept by Bruno Gentili: plays constructed from previously existing plays.[26] He distinguishes this definition based on the history of a text's creation sharply from a literary critic's definition of a play-within-the-play motif in a text. The two definitions are indeed hermeneutically distinct, but a central thesis of this work will be that, at least in Plautus, they are phenomenologically related.

I shall define metatheatre as theatrically self-conscious theatre, i.e., theatre that demonstrates an awareness of its own theatricality. Comic theatre, *pace* Abel, was capable of such an awareness long before the Renaissance. Jokes about the play as play go back to Aristophanes, where they tend to be isolated phenomena. Plautine drama is full of references to the play as play and to the performers as players and playwrights.[27]

The concept of metatheatre is further related to Styan's category of non-illusory drama. Not all non-illusory drama is metatheatrical, but all metatheatre is to some degree non-illusory. Insofar as theatre

[23] Abel (1963), 83. Perhaps the best discussion of metatheatre in Abel, who sometimes tends toward the epigrammatic, is his essay "Metatheatre: Shakespeare and Calderon," 59-72.

[24] Abel (1963), 60.

[25] Although it is implicit in Abel that a new consciousness during the Renaissance made metatheatre possible, in fact he states that Shakespeare succeeded in creating metatheatre where neither Moliere nor Marlowe had before him because "Shakespeare was the only one possessed by a complete confidence in the power of the imagination. . . ." (Abel [1963], 64.) I shall argue that Plautus' belief in the power of the imagination was as remarkable.

[26] Gentili (1979), 15.

[27] Abel insists that metatheatre is not comedy, but the best answer to this is to be found in Kerr (1967), 269-73. See also Sontag (1966), 132-39; on metatheatrical aspects of comedy, see especially 135-36.

14

becomes self-conscious and aware of its own processes, it ceases to be strictly illusory. As the theatre games become ever cleverer and cleverer, the object of the audience's admiration becomes the dramatic skill, not the illusion. The conventions of Plautine theatre (the monologue, the aside, role-playing, the play-within-the-play) are by nature non-illusory, but it remains to be seen in what ways the uses of those conventions become metatheatrical.

A convention evolves because a specific device succeeds as dramatic communication. As the device solidifies into a pattern, it becomes as much an object for comedy as any other pattern or order. Just as comedy is the critic and opponent of rigid social order, so too it becomes the opponent of its own artistic order. Pseudolus tells us:

> nam qui in scaenam provenit,
> novo modo novom aliquid inventum adferre addecet.
>
> (568-69)

A man who takes the stage ought to bring on some new discovery, in newest style.

Novelty is essential for comedy, even when the basis of the comic world is that there is no new thing under the sun. Comedy must perpetually remake itself to remain fresh and alive. Otherwise it degenerates into sentimentality.

Indeed the conventions of comedy alone cannot stabilize the form forever. Comedy's penchant for turning its humor on itself and its own structures raises three possibilities. First, as I have just suggested, comedy can suppress its self-consciousness in favor of a sentimental repetition of the conventionalized form; no challenge to the conventions is acknowledged. Second, the self-conscious challenge, vigorously pursued, can empty the conventions of their original power and meaning, leaving only an ironic shell behind.[28] The

---

[28] This may indeed be what happens to Roman comedy in the hands of Terence. His challenge to both comic form and the society represented in comedy is deeply ironic. See, e.g., the readings of *Phormio* and *Hecyra* in Konstan (1983), a work I have seen only in the final stages of revising my own.

third possibility, and the one I argue Plautus was able to achieve, is for self-consciousness to be integrated into the very nature of the work; the result is metatheatre.

Plautus' remarkable achievement is to include self-conscious awareness of theatrical convention in a new concept of comic heroism, which I believe emerges most clearly in performance. A number of Plautus' characters, usually the clever slaves (*servi callidi*) but occasionally others very similar to them, demonstrate a self-awareness of the play as play and through this awareness demonstrate their own ability to control other characters in the play. The readings which follow are arranged in a loose progression to illustrate such a development in the power and range of Plautus' leading characters.

The clever slave characters certainly have not lacked for critical attention in the past, whether they were praised for their boisterous humor or condemned for spoiling the perfection of the Greek plays into which they were insinuated. Their character and actions, though, have most often been analyzed for signs of Plautine originality in language or plot function. Their sheer theatrical impact, in particular as onstage presence controlling the action, is too often either assumed to be obvious or ignored.

Crucial to this ability to control other characters is the power of improvisation. While other characters usually remain trapped in the stock roles to which their plot functions assign them, the clever slaves have the self-transformational power of the *versipellis* (skin-changer). They may themselves adopt one of the other stock roles of Roman comedy. Leonida in the *Asinaria*, for example, creates the role of the imperious overseer Saurea in order to swindle the merchant of his money. More importantly, though, the improvisational lead player knows how to use the humours and foibles of the other stock characters to bend them to his schemes. Chrysalus in the *Bacchides* knows precisely how old Nicobolus thinks (or perhaps does not think) when he is angry and therefore has the real control in the situation.[29]

[29] All of this is remarkably parallel to what Stephen Greenblatt in his chapter on "The Improvisation of Power" suggests is new in the European Renaissance personality: Greenblatt (1980), 222ff. He defines improvisation (not merely in the theatre but in all of life's dealings) as ". . . the ability to transform given materials into one's own scenario" and demonstates ". . . the Europeans' ability

In some plays this improvisational control is sporadic or diffuse. The *Asinaria* is pulled in as many different directions as there are players, while in the *Bacchides* control of the inner and outer plays is vested in Chrysalus and the two sisters respectively. Characters in some of Plautus' plays not discussed here also demonstrate on occasion similar improvisational control. It is in the six plays here discussed in detail, though, that Plautus best integrates this improvisational ability with self-consciousness of form.

Because improvisational control relies so heavily on the non-textual elements of theatre, it can best be appreciated through a performance approach to the plays. The eavesdropper on the page is a virtual cipher; on stage he is a powerful presence, coloring and

---

again and again to insinuate themselves into the preexisting political, religious, even psychic structure of the natives and to turn those structures to their advantage" (p. 227). Substitute "other characters" for "natives," and one has an excellent definition of what an improvisational hero in Plautus is able to do. Greenblatt suggests that ". . . improvisation is made possible by the subversive perception of another's truth as an ideological construct" (p. 228). Pseudolus, Chrysalus, and the others base their power on the ability to manipulate others as *artistic* constructs.

Improvisation and metatheatre seem to me intimately related. Greenblatt supplies a detailed study of the cultural background that Abel assumes for Renaissance metatheatre. The question of the cultural background to Plautus' metatheatre thus immediately arises. It is a question worth serious consideration but cannot be treated in detail here. My primary purpose it to explicate Plautus as a theatrical phenomenon. I can here only record my belief that the "mobile sensibility" which Greenblatt speaks of in the Renaissance was *not* generalized in Roman culture. This "mobile sensibility" implies a certain alienation from culture. Plautus, as an Umbrian, was uniquely well placed to perceive both Roman and Greek cultures as ideological constructs. His experience of theatre and role-playing could only reinforce this perception. Greenblatt again (p. 228): ". . . we may ask ourselves what conditions exist in Renaissance culture that make such an improvisation possible. It depends first upon the ability and willingness to play a role, to transform oneself, if only for a brief period and with mental reservation, into another. This necessitates the acceptance of disguise, the ability to effect a divorce, in Ascham's phrase, between the tongue and the heart. Such role-playing in turn depends upon the transformation of another's reality into a manipulable fiction." All of these conditions are implicit in Plautus' theatrical background—but not that of the Romans at large. We may note parenthetically that most classicists would automatically ascribe "Ascham's phrase" to Euripides—but Euripidean metatheatre should be the subject of another book.

shaping our perception of the scene and characters he overhears even when not commenting aside. Improvisation may proceed by fits and starts; as narrative text, such false starts and interrupted action may seem awkward indeed, yet such an approach comes alive in performance.

Far from being the hack translator depicted in nineteenth-century scholarship, Plautus is a superb comic craftsman who remakes his genre in many ways. No one would accuse him of being an exponent of the well-made play—but there are precious few comedies worthy of the name which are well-made plays. We may find in the following plays that in remaking comedy Plautus has not always achieved an integrated vision of the individual play. Even then he will not need my defense, for all these plays leave us laughing as they go. Let the prologue cease and the plays begin.

CHAPTER II

Epidicus

One look at the average audience gives us an irresistible urge to assault it—to shoot first and ask questions later.
—Peter Brook, *The Empty Space*

THE *Epidicus* offers us a convenient starting-point for the study of non-illusory convention and metatheatre in Plautus. The play is short and tightly focussed on the title character. Epidicus is one of the best and most straightforward examples of the stock clever slave, the *servus callidus*. He is the type against which the variations we will find in other plays play. Perhaps most important, the play was one of Plautus' own favorites.

The play has not been popular recently, yet Plautus himself evidently regarded it as one of his great successes, if we are to hear the poet's voice in that of Chrysalus in the *Bacchides* when he speaks of:

> etiam Epidicum, quam ego fabulam aeque ac me ipsum
> amo. . . .   (214)

and *Epidicus*, a play I love as much as I love myself. . . .[1]

Was Plautus, the first playwright to support himself solely by his art, for once radically wrong? Yet his allusion in the *Bacchides* is not defensive but rather holds the play up as a model. He could not have so far mistaken his immediate audience's reaction, at least.

---

[1] I am irresistibly reminded of a line from the Modern Major General's song in *Pirates of Penzance*, where he says he can "whistle all the airs from that infernal nonsense *Pinafore*." Gilbert's allusion to his previous work is not merely self-advertisment. If *HMS Pinafore* had not been a popular success (as well as an artistic one), the joke would have fallen flat. We are likewise entitled to speculate that *Epidicus* must have been a popular success as well for the allusion in *Bacchides* to have any point.

Not one piece of what might properly be called literary criticism of the *Epidicus* (as opposed to *Quellenforschung*) has appeared in this century. Instead every mind has been occupied with the problem of the Greek original—with modest results. No identification of a source has won widespread support. Indeed, the most persuasive study of the question has suggested there may be no original: Sander M. Goldberg in a recent article has made a strong case for the *Epidicus* as an essentially free Plautine composition.[2] Goldberg sees the play as a celebration of the eponymous slave hero. That view in itself is unexceptionable, but the techniques through which Plautus achieves this effect deserve more careful consideration. If indeed this is a free Plautine creation, there can hardly be a more important text in the corpus.

The play opens without prologue, a fact that has occasioned a great deal of critical controversy.[3] We shall defer until the end a discussion of whether on internal grounds such a prologue is dramaturgically necessary. For now let us examine the text as it stands. Instead of a prologue we have a dispute between two slaves, Thesprio, who has just returned with his young master Stratippocles from the siege and sack of Thebes, and Epidicus, the *servus callidus*. A similar scene opens the *Mostellaria*. There are, however, some differences of which we should be aware. First of all, the *Epidicus* opens in an elaborate *canticum*, while the *Mostellaria* employs the conversational iambic senarii.[4] Second, the *Mostellaria* scene gives us all the essential information that a prologue would have provided. That in the *Epidicus* is primarily a scene of banter between the two slaves, though we do learn that young Stratippocles is not only bringing home a

---

[2] Goldberg (1978), 81-91. Goldberg was not aware of an article by Katsouris (1977), 316-24, who with breathtaking insouciance derives the title *Homopatrioi* from *Epidicus* 642: *alia matra, uno patre*, and then argues for the Menandrean work of this title as the original of the *Epidicus*. Even assuming the existence of a Greek original at all (which Goldberg shows we need not do), Katsouris has only "techniques and motifs" that he himself admits "are not exclusively Menandrean" (p. 324) upon which to base his identification—hardly satisfactory. Dingel (1978) argues for Menander rather than Webster's suggestion of Apollodorus of Karystos.

[3] Best summarized in the edition of Duckworth (1940), 97-99, 207, 208, which provides consistent illumination on the problems of this play.

[4] Cantica are a sign of Plautine reworking. See Fraenkel (1960), 307-53.

pretty female captive from the war but also has one already at home provided by Epidicus' wiles. It requires the further illumination provided by Epidicus' monologue (81ff.) to explain that Epidicus has obtained the girl already at home by convincing Stratippocles' father that she is in fact his daughter. Indeed, this speech, more than the opening scene, functions as the delayed prologue.

This monologue (81-103) offers us a fascinating study in many ways, but particularly for its depiction of the transition from non-illusory modes of playing to the illusory. The scene that precedes it could open virtually any Plautine play. Information is conveyed but no action undertaken. Thesprio at least is not so much a character as a mouthpiece; the rest of the play manages quite nicely without him.

Epidicus is another matter, as his speech now shows. Formally there is no direct address to the audience: the monologue is framed as a schizophrenic internal dialogue. This is emphatic from the beginning (after one incorporated stage direction, 81 *illic hinc abiit*). Epidicus is talking to himself, as line 82 shows in three ways: by the use of the vocative in the emphatic position, the *tibi*, and the emphatic form of the accusative in *tete*. This monologue deserves to be studied in full, as some very curious things are going on here:

> *solus nunc es. quo in loco haec res sit vides*
> *Epidice. nisi quid tibi in tete auxili est, absumptus es.*
> *tantae in te impendent ruinae. nisi suffulcis firmiter,*
> *non potes subsistere, itaque in te ruont montes mali.*

> Neque ego nunc
> quo modo
> me expeditum ex impedito faciam consilium placet.
> ego miser
> pepuli
> meis dolis senem, ut censeret suam sese emere filiam.
> is suo
> filio
> fidicinam emit quam ipse amat, quam abiens mandavit mihi.

> Si sibi nunc
> alteram

ab legione abduxit animi causa, corium perdidi.
 nam ubi senex
 senserit
sibi data esse verba, virgis dorsum depoliet meum.
 at enim tu
 praecave.
at enim—*bat enim! nihil est istuc. plane hoc corruptumst caput.*

 Nequam homo es,
 Epidice.
qui lubidost male loqui? *quia tute tete deseris.*
 quid faciam?
 men rogas?
tuquidem antehac aliis solebas dare consilia mutua.
aliquid aliqua reperiumdumst. sed ego cesso ire obviam
adulescenti, ut quid negoti sit sciam. atque ipse illic est.
(81-101)

(Now you're alone. You see the spot you're in, Epidicus. Unless you've a trick up your sleeve, you're all washed up. There's a great crash coming for you. If you don't really brace yourself, you'll never stand up to it, and then mountains of misfortune will overwhelm you.)

Now I don't know how to extricate myself from these intricacies. I've so confounded the old man that he thinks he's bought his own daughter. In fact he bought his son the flute girl the boy's in love with—and the boy went and left her in my charge! Now if he's brought another girl home from the army—I've lost my hide! When the old fellow finds how he's fooled, he'll birch my back clean.

(But you, beware.) Yes, but. . . . *(But what?! There's nothing to that! What a born loser! You're a worthless fellow, Epidicus.)*

Why do you want to abuse me? *(Because you deserve it.)*

What shall I do? *(You're asking me?! You always used to have advice to lend. Somehow something must be found.)*

But I must waylay the boy, to learn what's up—and there he is!

This dialogue is as hilarious as it is conceptually fascinating. Who are these two voices? It is clear that the *tu* is Epidicus; he is twice so addressed in the vocative (82 and 96). Who is the other voice, the voice that addresses the *tu*? We cannot yet tell. For the sake of simplicity, then, let us refer to them as Epidicus and the other voice.

In the excerpt above I have indicated the division between the two voices by italicizing the lines to be attributed to the other voice. The other voice dominates the discussion in tone; it is both imperious and censorious. It begins the discussion with a harsh warning (81-84). Epidicus is allowed the exposition, but what he says seems to anger the other voice, and the interjections become even sharper: *at enim tu praecave!* Poor Epidicus is now limited to a trisyllabic protest (*at enim*), a question in rather hurt tones (*qui lubidost male loqui?*), and an open appeal (*quid faciam?*). The latter prompts one of the more exquisite exchanges in Plautus, a character asking himself: "What shall I do?" "You're asking *me?*"

But we still do not know exactly what is going on in this brief and tantalizing passage. The key to interpreting it lies in the playing. We cannot be certain how the actor in the second century B.C. solved the problem. Nonetheless, we can recognize it as a problem and recognize that all playable solutions will have certain things in common.

The basic challenge to the actor is to differentiate between the two voices. If the actor does nothing to mark his change from one voice to another, the audience will soon become confused and the humor lost. This point is easily lost in the reading where the reader, if he momentarily loses track of what is happening, can always go back a few lines and try to pick up the thread again. It is never possible for the audience to go back.

The differentiation between the two voices could literally be vocal: the performer could alter the pitch or timbre of his voice in such a way as to make two personalities distinctly emerge. But we are still left somewhat in doubt. One personality is Epidicus. He is so addressed, and presumably the performer used the same voice he would for the character of Epidicus throughout the play. We still do not know *who* the other voice is.

I suggest that this scene may be treated as a dialogue between the player and his mask. Nothing in the previous scene has yet shown

Epidicus as the intriguing slave. The crisis has come, but he has still to rise to meet it. Where does the strength to meet it come from? It comes from the persona, from the very mask of the intriguing slave character. Just this sort of thing happened in the commedia dell' arte: "In a drama of spontaneity and improvisation before a fully participating audience, the mask animates the body, and in turn the body further defines the expression of the mask. . . ."[5] The actor might at the beginning of this soliloquy remove his mask and address it as Epidicus.[6] The other voice, then, is the actor's own, admonishing the character of Epidicus, reminding the mask of its nature as a character. In speaking of the actor here I do not of course refer to the original player of two millennia gone. I mean simply the player as unmarked identity, the player who has not yet adopted a role. On any hypothesis the other voice is not the voice of the character Epidicus. Here we encounter the sense of pseudo-improvisation that Plautus so often cultivates, a sense in the tradition of the Atellan farce or the commedia. The action seems to flow spontaneously from the character/mask, not from the player's or the playwright's previous instructions. The player here has no course of action to propose to Epidicus. He merely says: *aliquid aliqua reperiundumst*, "somehow something must be found" (100).[7] No matter—the animated character of Epidicus himself is enough to carry the action forward. He has now talked himself into his role, much as Phronesium talks herself into the role of recently delivered mother in the *Truculentus*.[8]

Now the play begins in earnest, and Stratippocles and Chaeribulus arrive on the scene. Epidicus withdraws (103 *huc concedam*) into a convenient doorway to eavesdrop. In doing so he aligns himself

---

[5] Styan (1975), 114.

[6] Whether or not this was the solution adopted by the Roman actor does not matter. Its claim to validity as an interpretation of the text rests on its playability. On the question of the use of masks, see the Introduction including n. 7.

[7] We will encounter later a nice ironic echo of this in 331-32, where Chaeribulus suggests: *verum aliquid aliqua aliquo modo / alicunde ab aliqui aliqua spes est fore meliorem fortunam*, "In truth somewhere somehow some way with someone's help there's some hope of better luck."

[8] *Truc.* 449ff. Here of course the move is from one role (*meretrix*) to another (mother), not as in *Epidicus* from without to within the play. Pinacium in the *Stichus* (274ff.) talks himself into the running-slave role in a similar fashion.

with the audience, for we both (Epidicus and audience alike) now focus on the play-within-the-play, the scene between the two young men. Though our sympathy for Epidicus may hardly need reinforcing at this point, his sharing a point of view with the audience is a structural means of such reinforcement. Before stepping into the action again, Epidicus shares an ironic joke with the audience. Stratippocles has just threatened the supposedly absent slave with fearful punishment (121-23) if the money he needs is not forthcoming. Epidicus drily remarks:

> salva res est: bene promittit, spero servabit fidem.
> sine meo sumptu paratae jam sunt scapulis symbolae.
>
> (124-25)

All's well. I hope he keeps his handsome promise. My shoulders will have a new mantle of blows at no expense to me.

This sharing a private joke with us reinforces both Epidicus' equality and camaraderie with us, the audience, and his superiority to the world of characters he is about to reenter. The scene reiterates the information we already have about Stratippocles' old and new loves. It is worth noting in passing that Epidicus plays *eiron* in the scene, pretending to less knowledge of the situation than he has (132 *nam qui perdidi* . . .). Stratippocles and Chaeribulus, satisfied that Epidicus will now take care of everything, exit to their pleasures.

Epidicus has one more monologue before he follows them off (158-65). What is its function? It gives us no more information. Rather it shows us once again that the action is being improvised as we go along. Epidicus must summon the senate in his heart to deal with the problem of getting the money:

> ite intro, ego de re argentaria
> jam senatum convocabo in corde consiliarium. . . . (158-59)

You go inside, while I convene the Senate Finance Committee in my heart. . . .

As lines 151-52 showed at the end of the last scene, with their string of indefinites echoing the vague commands of the other voice in 100, Epidicus still has no definite plan in mind for obtaining the money, but such is his stature in the eyes of the two young men that they accept his assurances freely (152-53 *plenus consili es. novi te ego.*). Once more the schizophrenic dialogue of actor and character resumes for a moment. The other voice urges immediate but un-specified action:

Epidice, vide quid agas, ita res subito haec objectast tibi;
non enim nunc tibi dormitandi neque cunctandi copia est.

(161-62)

Epidicus, this problem has hit you so fast, you'd better
watch what you're doing. Now you don't have the luxury of
dozing or dawdling.

It is Epidicus (163 *mihi*) who decides, perfectly in character, to tackle old Periphanes. Thus the character, not the actor, makes the decision—but what is the decision? For a moment Epidicus may seem not equal to the audience but superior, because he seems to have a plan he does not share with us.

Lines 168 and following introduce us to Periphanes, the father of Stratippocles, and his friend Apoecides. We learn that Periphanes' conscience, perhaps prompted by his supposed recovery of his daughter, is bothering him, and he is thinking of marrying the girl's mother. Plautus, however, is careful not to throw too much emphasis on this point. By relating this information through the friend, Apoecides, he leaves Periphanes' commitment to this course of action in doubt. Indeed, Periphanes' only line on the subject expresses doubt: 172 *revereor filium.*[9]

Now Epidicus, unnoticed by the two old men, regains the stage. His imagery of auspices and a knife to disembowel not the sacrifice

---

[9] This plan to marry Philippa, which is never referred to again in the play, has offered great joy and comfort to critics who are sure Plautus must always translate and botch his translations. We are *not* entitled to imagine a New Comedy original in which Periphanes married Philippa in the finale from such scant evidence.

but Periphanes' purse (181-83) paints him in the typical military colors of the *servus gloriosus*, since auspices are taken before a military campaign. More importantly, as an unnoticed eavesdropper on the play-within-the-play, he again aligns himself with the audience's point of view and sympathies.

Here the high-speed improvisation begins. A chance recommendation of Apoecides, that Periphanes should marry off his son at once (190), gives Epidicus the opening he needs. He sees his course of action immediately (192ff.), though we are not let in on the details yet. Once more he instructs himself on playing a role, even down to details of costume:[10]

> age nunciam orna te, Epidice, et palliolum in collum conice
> itaque adsimulate quasi per urbem totam hominem
>   quaesiveris.
> age, si quid agis.   (194-96)

> Come on, Epidicus, outfit yourself. Cast your cloak back and act as if you've chased the man through the whole city.
> Come on, let's see some acting.

He will make himself into the *servus currens*. Such improvisation is intimately associated with the assumption of a role.[11] Once in his new role, Epidicus is free, indeed inspired, to invent the whole scheme.

The scene that follows (196ff.) makes one wonder if Plautus' characters, just like those of Dickens, did not talk to him and even run away with the story line in directions the author did not intend. Once again, Epidicus is superior to us, the audience, because we are as much in the dark about the tale he will tell as the old men are. After Epidicus shows us how well he can perform the role of breathless *servus currens*, he produces the first piece of news (this in

---

[10] Costume is an intimate part of the assumption of a role. Phronesium (see n. 8 above) in the *Truculentus* (463-64) comments on her costuming as part of her assumption of the mother role. The prologue in the *Poenulus* announces at the end that he must go and put his costume on (123 *ego ibo, ornabor*) as part of his assumption of a role in the play.

[11] Styan (1975), 149.

fact accurate; note how skillfully Epidicus embroiders and alters the truth): the army is back. Then his imagination takes wing and the scene, with returning soldiers, pack animals, booty, and the welcoming crowd, grows in our minds. After the bait, the hook: he claims to have seen young Stratippocles' mistress waiting for him. A chance detail about the finery she was wearing prompts Periphanes to ask a question (223), and Epidicus in his eagerness to show that he *has* seen all this nearly derails the discussion with a discursus on fashion (224ff.). He and Plautus share a delight in the music of names that carries them away here.

Epidicus now proceeds to create a fictitious conversation between two bystanders he says he overheard (236ff.). Earlier he has been setting the scene with description. Now he begins to resemble a playwright as he invents dialogue for these bystanders. Epidicus' invention is working rapidly but barely fast enough to keep up with the impatience of his listeners, to judge by the interruptions of Periphanes, who first expresses his desire to hear all (240) and then jumps in when Epidicus slows or pauses in his tale with a quick interrogative (241 *quid?*). Epidicus buys time by complaining of the interruption (241 *tace ergo, ut audias*), then springs the trap: Stratippocles has already borrowed money from a Theban moneylender to buy and free his mistress (deftly composed of half-truths).

Periphanes swallows this tale whole and is therefore perfectly ready to adopt any plan Epidicus proposes—too ready in fact. Epidicus seems to expect resistance and finds none; Periphanes is demanding particulars before Epidicus is ready to give them:

> EP. si aequom siet
>   me plus sapere quam vos, dederim vobis consilium catum
>   quod laudetis, ut ego opino, uterque—
> PER.   Ergo ubi id est,
>   Epidice?
> EP. atque ad eam rem conducibile.
> AP.   quid istuc dubitas dicere?
>   (257-60)

EP. If it were proper that I should know more than you, I'd give you a plan so clever you'd praise it, or so I think. And then. . . .

PER. Well, what is it, Epidicus?
EP. Also useful for the matter at hand.
AP. Why hesitate to say it?

Epidicus' hesitation here is usually interpreted as mock humility.[12] Rather it is once more a demonstration of the improvisatory character of Epidicus' plan. He cleverly makes Periphanes believe that this is only modesty, stalling for seven lines (260-66). The plan he finally puts forth is the one he has overheard Apoecides recommend: to marry young Stratippocles off (267).

This plan is somewhat vague and still evolving. Periphanes presses for details (274 *quin tu eloquere, quid faciemus?*). What Epidicus now comes up with is based—naturally—on role-playing: in this case, Periphanes is to play *senex amator* (274-76)! After an initial protest Periphanes falls in with the scheme—again, a little too readily. Once more he presses for details: 285 *rem hercle loquere*, 286 *sine me scire*. Perhaps up until this point Epidicus *had* planned to take Periphanes himself to the slave-dealer, but the old man is proving to be a little sharper than he should be, so one final refinement is added: Apoecides will act as agent for Periphanes (287-91). The final arrangements about money are made, and the old men depart.

By now we can see that Epidicus' plot is a continually evolving improvisation. He invents scenes, characters, and dialogue with equal ease. In the scene just past he twice had to recover from unexpected eagerness on the part of Periphanes, but these abortive challenges to his control of the plot have been successfully dealt with. Indeed, his skill at improvising increases our respect for him. His soliloquy before he pursues Periphanes into the house has yet one more improvisation—where and how to find a girl to play the part of the son's mistress. Like all good liars, Epidicus weaves as much of the truth as he can into his plots: before, the Theban moneylender and the return of the army; now, the flute girl, requested, he informs us, by the *senex* to play for a sacrifice.

The following scene (320-36) functions as counterpoint and breathing-space after the long, virtually continuous buildup of action under the direction of Epidicus. Indeed, his presence has grown almost oppressive. We are nearly halfway through the play, and

[12] Cf. Duckworth (1940), 256, *ad* 257-66; Segal (1968), 215, n. 50.

the title character has been offstage for only 15 lines (166-80) up until now. Stratippocles and Chaeribulus have begun to despair of Epidicus' success and have fallen to quarrelling. The principal object of the scene is to render Epidicus' triumphant return more striking.[13]

Epidicus returns to his own victory strains (337ff.). It is worth noting that the two voices are now gone for good; the character mask is firmly in place. All his lines are now in the first person. He sees Stratippocles and Chaeribulus, hands over the money, and details one last scene of improvisational theatre he intends to enact, a scene in which none of the other participants (the *leno*, the *fidicina*, and Apoecides) will really know what is going on. Epidicus has a little coaching of two of the participants yet to do:

> deveniam ad lenonem domum egomet solus, eum ego
> docebo. . . .   (364)

I'll go down to the pimp's house all by myself, I'll instruct him. . . .

> jam ego parabo
> aliquam dolosam fidicinam. . . .   (371-72)

Now I'll ready some tricky flute-girl. . . .

The spring of the plot is now wound tight; its unwinding comes rapidly and straightforwardly, and we can deal with it in fairly short order. Periphanes' self-congratulatory musings on his new wisdom in dealing with his son are interrupted by the return of Apoecides

---

[13] Such scenes of fear while an issue is being decided offstage are common in Plautus, as in other comedy. According to Beckerman (1971), 80-87, such scenes are "reactive." The "project" or purpose of such a scene is for the participants to adjust emotionally to the dreaded state of affairs. In tragedy, of course, these projects of adjustment can succeed; Beckerman's example is Electra mourning over the supposed urn of her brother Orestes. In comedy, however, which Beckerman does not treat, such scenes do not lead to an emotional adjustment; the "project" fails. This is a reflection on a small scale of Walter Kerr's larger assertion in *Tragedy and Comedy* (New York, 1967) that comedy is about limitations. Comic characters are too limited to adjust to disaster. It merely happens to them.

and the flute girl. All has gone according to plan, so much so that Apoecides returns full of Epidicus' praises (410-11). In passing, one ominous note is struck: a passerby told Apoecides that Stratippocles was back in town (407-8). It is a tiny point, but Epidicus' earlier assertion that Stratippocles would not be back until the next day (272-73) is disproved. This foreshadows Periphanes' chance meetings with the Euboean soldier and Philippa, which will unravel the whole of Epidicus' scheme.

Periphanes' scene with the Euboean soldier (437-92), which moves swiftly to the revelation that the flute girl is *not* Acropolistis, Stratippocles' mistress, is enlivened by one striking character note: Periphanes is an old *miles glorious*![14] Consequently he is unwilling to listen to the Euboean's long-winded boasts (453-55) and demands that they get down to business at once. He strikes a perfectly good deal with the soldier which blows up in his face over the minor technicality that the flute girl is not Acropolistis.

Now—was the flute girl in on Epidicus' scheme or not? She *says* she was merely hired to play for a sacrifice (500-1). Some have assumed this means that Epidicus, contrary to his intentions stated earlier, did not let her in on the scheme but duped her as well.[15] It could be that Epidicus, ever the improviser, changed his plans after all. The more likely (and more dramatically interesting) explantion is that she has no motivation to reveal the whole truth. Epidicus, as Periphanes' representative, has hired her to play—but what? If she says she was hired to play the flute, she can also play dumb and innocent—no part of any fraudulent sale. Indeed, she has a motive for *not* telling the truth therein.[16] She simply joins in the spirit of Plautine fun by also deluding the old man.

We have not long to wait for the other shoe to drop. Philippa, the mother of Telestis, arrives on the scene and sets in motion the

---

[14] I accept Leo's transfer of lines 431-34 to a position after 455, thus confining this revelation to the scene with the *miles*. Duckworth (1940), 322-23, accepts the lines in the position transmitted in the manuscripts and regards them as a bridge between the two scenes. Dramatically it is far more effective to have the revelation of Periphanes' past pop up only when needed—but this is admittedly not proof.

[15] E.g., Wheeler (1917), 237-64.

[16] This is substantially the explanation Duckworth (1940), 277-79, adopts, though he stresses realistic logic rather than dramatic logic.

final exposure of Epidicus' improvisations (526ff.). Periphanes spots her first, and Plautus creates an elaborate, choreographed sequence whereby they approach, fence, and finally recognize each other.[17] This is a splendid bit of non-illusory comedy. Both characters are in close communication with the audience but not yet with each other (533-47).[18] Each bids for the audience's sympathy while advancing on the other with all the courage of a Sir Andrew Aguecheek. Philippa wins the encounter by forcing Periphanes to confess first that he is the man who wronged her (558 *ego sum*), but then breaks down and has to be comforted by Periphanes. The comfort she seeks, the reassurance that her daughter is safe (567 *fac videam*), precipitates the revelation.

Periphanes attempts to stage the proper recognition scene between mother and daughter that would end their little domestic tragicomedy. He even gives the stage direction that the two women should kiss (571). Unfortunately for him, the play turns out to have been written by Epidicus (592 *Epidicus mihi fuit magister*),[19] not him, and his sentimental tragedy turns into farce. The girl is revealed as a fraud, the mother left disconsolate, and Periphanes goes off in a rage.

The collapse of tragedy into comedy is brought about by the fluidity of identity and role. Acropolistis' speech shows this best:

> tua istaec culpast, non mea.
> non patrem ego te nominem, ubi tu tuam me appelles filiam?
> hanc quoque etiam, si me appellet filiam, matrem vocem.
> negat haec filiam me suam esse: non ergo haec mater mea
>> est.
> postremo haec mea culpa non est: quae didici dixi omnia;
> Epidicus mihi fuit magister.   (587-92)

---

[17] ". . . thoroughly Plautine . . ." says Goldberg (1978), 86-87. He also compares Plautus' expansion of such an approach in *Bacchides*, 534-35.

[18] Two characters, each speaking aside to the audience with reference to the other, are by no means unknown in Plautus (cf. Demipho and Charinus in *Mercator* 378ff.), but the sequence is usually not extended.

[19] The teaching metaphor for instructing actors is alive in Latin as well as in Greek. Cf. 364 above. We need not assume, however, that it translates a Greek *didaskein* here. The conceit is more likely to be Plautus' own.

It's your fault, not mine. Should I not call you father, when
you address me as your daughter? I'd call this lady "mother"
too, if she would call me daughter. She says I'm not her
daughter; very well, then, she's not my mother. It's really
not my fault: I said all the lines I learned. Epidicus was my
coach.

She is willing to be a player, to have her role assigned to her. Her
identity is determined by whoever is the playwright of her play, in
this case Epidicus.[20] She implies that Periphanes' identity and role
are equally subject to change, indeed at his own wish:

ubi voles pater esse ibi esto; ubi noles ne fueris pater.   (595)

If you want to be "daddy," so be it; if you don't, don't!

Periphanes' problem is that he is not a successful playwright
like Epidicus. If he were, he could create himself in his chosen
image, just as Epidicus has.

The fifth act opens in a reversal of the opening of the third
(607ff.)[21] Stratippocles is in high spirits, Epidicus in despair and
in need of comfort from his master (618 *habe bonum animum*, 619
ego te servabo). As in the earlier scene, the temporary despair serves
to heighten the pleasure of peripety. The moneylender arrives with
Telestis, whom Epidicus recognizes as the daughter of his old master
(634ff.). With this piece of good fortune, Epidicus' doubts and
fears are at an end; his knowledge of the girl's identity restores his
power in the play. Once more he is in control of the scene; note his
imperatives in 643, 652, 655, 658, and 660.

Some have found the resolution of the play by this chance

[20] One might compare the delightful exchange reported in Mary Chase's
Harvey. Elwood P. Dowd reports meeting Harvey under a lamppost. When
he asks Harvey's name, Harvey asks him what name he likes. Elwood says,
"Harvey," and Harvey replies that by a remarkable coincidence that happens
to be *his* name.

[21] I do not propose to discuss again the question of act divisions in Roman
comedy. The position of Duckworth (1952), 98-101, that action was *generally*
continuous seems irrefutable. However, the occurrences of an empty stage

recognition unsatisfactory.[22] It is, however, perfectly in keeping with the improvisatory nature of the action so far. Epidicus works with the material to hand. The building-blocks of his tricks are "real" people and events, suitably rearranged: the Theban money-lender, the flute girl/mistress, the capture of the daughter, the return of the army from Thebes. Something he can use always does turn up for Epidicus, unlike poor Mr. Micawber. His renewed grip on the helm of the play is best signalled by a line in his exiting soliloquy:

eadem haec intus edocebo quae scio Stratippoclem.   (662)

I'll rehearse inside what I know with Stratippocles.

He is back to coaching others in their parts.

The final scene (666ff.) repeats a pattern we have seen often in this play. The old men enter worn out from hunting Epidicus (and Telestis too, it seems, though this point is brushed over). Epidicus enters unnoticed a few lines later (675). By stepping at first only to the edge of the magic playing circle, as it were, Epidicus shares once again the superiority of the audience to the characters fully within the play; he at first ignores the old men, as he exults to the audience in the overthrow of his enemies.

Stepping into the circle, Epidicus taunts the old men into a fury with his demands to be bound by them (680ff.). His sheer self-confidence makes them fearful of a trap (690 *nescioquam fabricam facit*). It is indeed a trap, for Periphanes, discovering that Epidicus has returned his daughter to him, is put in the degrading position of begging his slave for forgiveness and buys that forgiveness only at the price of the slave's liberty—a gift Epidicus accepts with reluctance!

---

before both line 328 and line 607 might encourage the spectators to draw the parallel.

[22] Undoubtedly Aristotle would not have approved (*Poetics* 1454b-55a). Even Goldberg (1978), 87, feels Plautus struggles "to obscure the fact that he [Epidicus] has escaped this final difficulty entirely by chance." I doubt Plautus worried about this at all. As Flaubert said in one of his letters to Louise Colet, "Plautus would have laughed at Aristotle had he known his rules . . ." [Steeg-muller (1980), 85].

PER. . . . at ob eam rem liber esto.
EP.   invitus do hanc veniam.
                                    (730)

PER. . . . but for that very reason be free.
EP. I'll do it reluctantly—as a favor.

Of the two-line epilogue we can say little:

Hic is homo est qui libertatem malitia invenit sua.
plaudite et valete. lumbos porgite atque exsurgite.   (732-33)

Here is a man who found freedom by his roguery.
Applaud then and farewell. Get up and stretch your legs.

The characters are dropped, but the play is not quite over. There is a "moral" (though it is really praise for *malitia*), an appeal for applause, and a joking bit of parting advice.

The action of the *Epidicus*, then, is one extended improvisation by the title character. It is a matter for some speculation to what extent Plautus aims at an imitation of the spontaneity of preliterary Atellan farce. Certainly the spirit of the piece is more in keeping with the commedia dell' arte tradition, which is arguably the descendant of the nonliterary Atellan farce.

Our discussion should answer one much debated question about the *Epidicus*: did it once have an expository prologue, now lost? The improvised *Epidicus* is the very opposite of static Menandrean drama, where an omniscient prologue like Fortuna can lay out the whole of the action before it commences.[23] The plot is generated by the fertile brain of Epidicus. It is not fixed but continuously coming to be.

[23] This is a matter of relative degree. The delayed prologue delivered by Tyche in the *Aspis* considerably reshapes our view of the play at that point. Still, the Menandrean prologue in general explicates. As Sander Goldberg says: "Menander usually uses a divine prologue speaker to colour our perceptions of his characters and situations and to shape our expectations, often by including a piece of information human characters do not know. . . . Divinities who speak prologues emphasize the distance between audience and actors . . ." [Goldberg (1980), 92].

We have met in *Epidicus* many of the non-illusory techniques of Plautine dramaturgy we shall see elsewhere: the aside, the monologue or soliloquy, the eavesdropping scene (and with it the play-within-the-play). There is also role-playing, though we might debate whether it is by nature metatheatrical. Epidicus, after his debate in the first soliloquy, adopts the role of the *servus callidus*. His only step out of this role thereafter is really into a subspecies, when he takes on the role of *servus currens*. The only major transference of role is merely alluded to in the play, having taken place through time beforehand: that of Periphanes from *miles* into *senex*. This is not key to the structure of the comedy, but it points the way to more complex transferrals and transformations in the *Asinaria* and *Casina*.

The continual improvisation, combined with a paucity of explicit references to the theatrical process, offers some support for Goldberg's suggestion that the *Epidicus* has no one Greek exemplar. There is no rhythm of action advancing the plot alternating with character business (the *lazzi* of commedia dell' arte) such as characterizes some of the plays discussed below. The fact that it is the shortest of the surviving plays is proof of its concentration on getting through the action.

The *Epidicus* is a play celebrating the powers of self-creation. Epidicus throws himself into the *servus callidus* role and thereby wins a mistress for his young master, a daughter for his old master, and freedom for himself. He does not really seem to want freedom, as Segal has pointed out.[24] Why? Because he is an artist, and, through his ability to create himself in any role he chooses, he has always been free.

[24] Segal (1968), 110-11.

CHAPTER III

The Ruse of Persia ∼ or ∼ The Story-Telling Slaves

THE fundamental paradox of the *Persa* is apparent from the very first line: an actor in a slave mask advances onto the stage and begins:

qui amans egens. . . .   (1)

The man who loves and lacks. . . .

The shock to the audience must have been marked. Could he be quoting his master? Could the actor in his haste lest he miss his entrance have grabbed the wrong mask? His costume would probably show the inanity of this assumption. No: by the time a first-person verb arrives in line 5, we realize that the slave, normally the witty critic of love, has himself fallen under its spell. His fellow slave Sagaristio will soon express no little surprise at this situation (25). The audience gropes to find a response, and no guidance for that response comes from the stage for some time.

It is usually said that in this introductory scene the slave Toxilus parodies the *adulescens amans*.[1] Parody, however, is a notoriously slippery term, all the more so in ancient literature. The unspoken, and I think unjustified, assumption is that the parody consists in putting noble sentiments on love in the mouth of a socially base character, a slave. The point would then be to ridicule those sentiments in the process—but is this Plautus' purpose here? We note first of all that these sentiments are not particularly noble: beneath the poetically elevated language comparing his trials to the labors of Hercules,[2] Toxilus is expressing distress at the state of his finances and not commenting directly on his feelings toward his beloved.

[1] Müller (1957), 3; Fraenkel (1960), 257.
[2] *Pace* Leo (1912), 151, the whole motif is thoroughly Plautine: see Fraenkel

At this point (7) another slave enters, Sagaristio. If Plautus were parodying the lover's extravagance, he would now have in Sagaristio the perfect mouthpiece for doing so. The audience could, through Sagaristio's attitude, be guided in its own response to the highly unusual character (Toxilus) now confronting it. In fact, Plautus seems to avoid the opportunity.[3]

(1960), 11. Netta Zagagi (1980), 15-67, has attempted recently to refute Fraenkel by seeking Greek sources other than the *Nea* for mythological hyperboles. It is possible that the great number of Hercules comparisons in Plautus owes something to the popularity of Hercules as a figure in South Italian farce, but in any case Plautus did not find this Hercules reference in his Greek original. Therefore its poetic functioning in the scene is his conscious artistic choice.

[3] Perhaps this is the place to deal with the only recent attempt at literary interpretation of the *Persa*, Guilbert (1962), 3-17. Beginning with the character of Toxilus but going on to other aspects as well, Guilbert contends that the whole play is a parody, a topsy-turvydom: Toxilus the slave takes on the role of the young master and lover and, although he is a slave, has a free man, the parasite Saturio, dependent upon him. Saturio himself, says Guilbert, is the reverse of our expectations: while the parasite is usually a young man dependent upon a young master, Saturio is middle-aged. The daughter, he further contends, is a parody in that, while she espouses high moral views, her own objections to the fraud the plotters are about to perpetrate on the slave-dealer are strictly self-interested: her reputation and prospects of marriage might be damaged. As parody, however, Toxilus is very flat. I shall argue below that he is an essay in quite a different type of character for Plautus, but for the moment it is sufficient to note that if he and the rest of the characters are intended as parody, they fail as such.

Menander shows us that strict parody of the *adulescens amans* was undertaken in New Comedy. We may compare a fragment of his *Hero* (lines cited from Sandbach's Oxford text [1972]). The scene takes place between Daos, the *servus amans*, and his fellow slave Getas. Getas' opening speech describes Daos' clear symptoms of distress: he has an expression of despair, is beating his head, tearing out his hair, and groaning (1-5). Eventually, Daos confesses the source of his woe: he is in love (15). Getas' irreverent response is to ascribe this condition to overeating (17). Getas, ever impudent, even manages to interject a joke into Daos' tale of the sad fall to penury of his lady love and her father's death (30-31). A little later Daos accuses Getas of laughing at him (39), and shortly thereafter the fragment breaks off. Although a good bit of this scene is devoted to exposition, even the restrained Menander extracts considerable humor from the *servus amans* as a figure of parody and fun.

By contrast in the first scene of the *Persa* opportunities for such humor seem deliberately avoided. The verbal gamesmanship that opens the dialogue could open virtually any encounter in Plautus and makes no reference to Toxilus'

Instead, Sagaristio guides the audience response in a different direction: he recalls Toxilus to his proper role, the role of the scheming *servus callidus*:

nimi' stulte amicis utere . . . imperare oportet.   (19)

You make a fool's use of your friends . . . you ought to give orders.

The word *imperare*, given the background of scheming slaves as military commanders, is a call to arms, a command to drop the *adulescens amans* persona and take up that of the *servus callidus*. Toxilus brightens enough to make a joke and continues the military imagery in the process (23). By line 24 Toxilus' military virtue is sufficiently aroused to see his love as battle:

saucius factus sum in Veneris proelio. . . .

I'm a casualty from the front lines of love. . . .

Soon he is beginning to do just what Sagaristio had suggested: give orders. Note the imperatives in 38, 43, 46, 47, 48, 50, and 51.

Toxilus began his exchange with Sagaristio in an inferior position, vacillating and helpless. In the course of the scene he undergoes a transformation that establishes his superiority, vividly marked by this exchange:

---

lovesickness (17-18). After a joke about punishment at the mill (21-23), Toxilus' confession that he is in love is an obvious opportunity for a scornful joke—but none comes. Even his comment at the end of the scene that love has made him a *morologus* (49) is not commented upon. Plautus is elsewhere perfectly able to exploit the comic spectacle of a man in love, as a glance at the opening of the *Pseudolus* (3-131) will show, but here he chooses not to do so.

I am therefore inclined to believe that no slave parody of the *adulescens amans* existed in the original—if an original existed. Plautus had a perfectly good eye for broad, parodistic humor. If it existed in a previous text, he cannot have failed to understand it. Either it did not exist, or he has chosen deliberately to suppress it in favor of a different artistic concept of the role. See below, 18.

SAG. Quid faciam?
TOX.   Rogas?
    alicunde exora mutuom.
SAG.   Tu fac idem quod
    rogas me.   (42-43)

SAG. What shall I do?
TOX. You're asking me? Beg a loan from somewhere.
SAG. *You* do it. It's your suggestion.

The exchange *quid faciam? rogas?* is strikingly reminiscent of *Epidicus* 98, where Epidicus is talking himself into his role. Sagaristio reminds Toxilus that he must be his own *servus callidus*. As imperatives begin to spring from his lips, we see that Toxilus is establishing himself as the mastermind of the plot, and cannot be bothered with details yet. Such a plot is further promised by his exit line:

usque ero domi dum excoxero lenoni malam rem aliquam.

(52)

Meanwhile I'll be home, cooking up a pot of trouble for the pimp.

Saturio, a parasite dependent on Toxilus, now enters and delivers a monologue. This monologue functions in two ways. It allows dramatic time for Toxilus' offstage completion of the process of character transformation. It also functions as a reassuring tonic note for the audience. Where Toxilus has profoundly disturbed our ideas of stock type, Saturio confirms them explicitly:

Veterem atque antiquom quaestum majorum meum
servo atque optineo et magna cum cura colo.   (53-54)

Ye old, right honorable calling of my ancestors I guard and keep and with great zeal pursue.

Saturio promises to be everything we expect a parasite to be. His lineage is pure parasite unto the sixth and seventh generations (56).

Jokes (e.g., 60) and popular criticism of informers (62ff.), which seem less than germane to us, are a reassertion of the comic world the audience knows and expects.[4]

The transformation from helpless lover to intriguing slave is complete when Toxilus returns: *omnem rem inveni* (81). He does not confide the details of his plot: indeed, we shall soon see they are still being improvised. He has no time, for he spots Saturio and moves into action at once.

In a quick aside he tells us how he will play the following scene (84 *similabo*). He creates a scene by a one-sided conversation with nonexistent offstage slaves designed to entice Saturio with a promise of food.[5] Toxilus, by the aside and his creativity, reverses the usual position of power in an eavesdropping scene. Usually the eavesdropper and the audience share the position of superior knowledge. Here Toxilus is in control of the dramatic communication, and the audience shares his position of knowledge.

Toxilus now reveals the plot he has conceived for his play by his request for the use of Saturio's daughter (127-64): he will have her sold to the slave-dealer, pocket the profits, and then allow Saturio to reclaim her as free. He must play firm military commander with Saturio (*exigam ego hercle te ex hac decuria* "I'll drum you right out of the corps!" 143) in order to get his way, but he succeeds.

Toxilus is creating improvisational theatre here. Note that he delegates some responsibilities for creating the tale to Saturio and his daughter:

praemostra docte, praecipe astu filiae
quid fabuletur: ubi se natam praedicet,
qui sibi parentes fuerint, und' surrupta sit.

---

[4] J. W. Halporn in a paper delivered at the 1980 meeting of the American Philological Association delineated a similar function for the parasite Ergasilus in the *Captivi*. There, as here, the parasite and his characterization anchor the play in the world of comedy when the unusual variations Plautus plays in the main plot may threaten to carry us away to a more serious world. Here, because the chief variation of the play is a stock type (the *servus* as *amator*), the acknowledgment of the parasite's role must be even more explicit than in the *Captivi*.

[5] Lines 85-98. Toxilus is working within the restraints of a limited troupe of players here, just as any Roman playwright would.

sed longe ab Athenis esse se gnatam autumet;
et ut adfleat quom ea memoret.   (148-52)

Instruct her cleverly, make it clear to the girl what tale to
spin, so she can say where she was born, who her parents
were, where she was abducted from. But she ought to say
she was born far from Athens—and weep when she
remembers.

He will also leave costume details to the *choregus*:

SAT. *pothen* ornamenta?
TOX.   aps chorago sumito;
    dare debet: praebenda aediles locaverunt.   (158-59)

SAT. Whence the costumes?
TOX. Get them from the producer—that's his job.
    The aediles assigned him to provide them.

The equation of Toxilus' play-within-the-play and the *Persa* itself is
vividly made in these two lines: both plays use the same *choregus*.[6]

If one can speak of comic relief within comedy, the two next
scenes between "masters" and slaves are prime examples. First we
meet Lemniselenis' self-important maid, Sophoclidisca, complaining
and almost abusing her mistress; this is immediately followed by a
scene of Toxilus and his personal slave Paegnium. The comic world
from which Saturio's monologue comes reasserts itself. This diver-
sion from the central problem of purchasing the freedom of Lemniselenis, Toxilus' *amica*, creates suspense; as Müller has noted,[7]
the dramatic effect of the play would be far weaker without this
"interruption." These speeches paint the characters who deliver them
in bold colors as well as articulating the main plot. The studied
contrast between the two scenes is worth noting as well. Whether

---

[6] The *choregus* was a familiar figure to Roman theatregoers; as evinced by
the humor of his appearance in the *Curculio* 462-86. There he plays wonderfully
with the nature of illusion and reality by wondering whether Curculio will steal
his costumes from him—a fiction grown so powerful that he can defraud reality!

[7] Müller (1957), 9.

one gives part of 179 to Lemniselenis or, as Lindsay does, leaves her entirely silent, her maid Sophoclidisca obviously dominates her scene (168-82). The helplessness of the heroine, and the relative activity and capability of the slave character, are thereby underscored. When Paegnium, the slave boy of Lemniselenis, arrives on stage, his scene on the other hand not only paints him as impudent but also shows us Toxilus in a new light (183-99). In his newly adopted role as master Toxilus must endure abuse from the slaves who serve him. There is nothing parodic in this portrayal of Toxilus as master; it merely exploits the humor of role reversal. The two messengers, Sophoclidisca and Paegnium, then meet, fence, bicker, and continue on their journeys (200-250) without materially advancing the plot—other than to establish that the two lovers are given to letter-writing. The action has stopped temporarily.

Sagaristio returns and in a joyous canticum (251-71) announces the gift that has dropped from the heavens: his master has given him money for a cattle-buying commission that he can now divert to Toxilus' purposes. His monologue is structurally isolated within the play, and I think to some purpose. Both Paegnium and Sophoclidisca have made long, emphatic crosses of the stage just before Sagaristio's appearance. Visually and verbally there is a sharp break. Both must cross back again (albeit not simultaneously this time) after Sagaristio's monologue, underscoring its isolation from the surrounding action. Plautus uses the opportunity of Paegnium's return to engage him in a scene of banter with Sagaristio (272-301). Delay is important. The impact of Sagaristio's announcement about the money diminishes with time.

The entrance of Toxilus and Sophoclidisca reminds us why Plautus has introduced this delay. Toxilus has prepared a plan of his own, on the basis of which he confidently reassures his mistress that all will be well (302-4). He has the power to continue the play without Sagaristio's help.

The rivalry between the two slaves for control of the plot and for the position of power within the play that such control implies underlies the whole of the scene. Sagaristio hopes to have a little fun with Toxilus, and confides to the audience how boastfully, with what a lordly manner he will play his scene bestowing help on Toxilus:

nunc huic ego graphice facetus fiam.
subnixis alis me inferam atque amicibor gloriose. (306-7)

Now I'll show him how clever I can be. I'll swagger up and
cloak myself in grandeur.

The scene does not quite have the tone Sagaristio wants, however.
It is indeed full of excellent humor, visual and verbal. Great attention
is paid to the position of the money pouch on Sagaristio's neck.
Eventually, though, Toxilus asserts his authority over the scene by
putting an end to the horseplay with *nimis tu facete loquere*, "You're
talking like a fool" (323). Toxilus is indeed grateful for the money,
but it can only change the timing, not the nature of his own plot to
defraud the slave-dealer. Sagaristio's bid for top billing has failed;
Toxilus remains the star:

> TOX. . . . nam jam omnis sycophantias instruxi et
> comparavi
> quo pacto ab lenone auferam hoc argentum—
> SAG.   tanto
> melior.
> TOX. et mulier ut sit libera atque ipse ultro det argentum.
> sed sequere me: ad eam rem usus est tua mihi
> opera.—
> SAG.   utere ut vis.   (325-28)

TOX. Now I've laid all my plans and devised a way to
separate the pimp from his money—
SAG. So much the better.
TOX. —and a way to free the girl, and he'll give me more
money yet. Now follow me—I need your help for this.
SAG. I'm at your disposal.

The ensuing scene between Saturio and his daughter (329-99)
shows us that Saturio has confided all he knows of the plot to
his daughter—and that is not much, to judge from her state of
confusion and trepidation. She does know, however, that she does

not want to be an actress: 358, *verum insimulari nolo*. The scene also
portrays her as a thoughtful and chaste character.[8] Father and daughter now exit into Toxilus' house, leaving the stage open for the next
confrontation.

Dordalus as villain of the piece is given a short entrance monologue (400-4) with one good joke in it that establishes his obsession
with money. Toxilus appears (405) and immediately begins his
verbal assault. Both he and Dordalus play this scene with one eye
on the audience; it is virtually a set insult contest on the order of
the *flagitatio* scene in the *Pseudolus* (359-69). Toxilus, in a reminder
that this is poetic drama, says he could not exhaust the catalogue of
the pimp's vices in three hundred verses:

> trecentis versibus
> tuas inpuritias traloqui nemo potest. . . .   (410-11)

> In three hundred verses no man could voice your vices. . . .

Dordalus catches his breath (417 *sine respirare me*) and bellows back
with matching bombast the vices of the slave "for all to hear" (426).
Indeed, he comes off rather better in the exchange; Toxilus grudgingly admires his lung power (427). Toxilus' suddenly placatory
attitude toward Dordalus may puzzle for a moment, but of course
he must now lay the groundwork for his scheme of the fraudulent
sale. He does, however, insist on the last word in the scene.

Toxilus' ensuing monologue (449-61) strikes the needed contrast to his manner toward Dordalus. His very act of retaining the
stage is a statement of strength. The spring of his plot is fully wound.
His observations on the success that attends the man who does his
work well and carefully reinforce his presence. He can look forward
to tying the pimp in knots (457 *intricatum dabo*), another plot-
weaving metaphor. He now calls for his props and players, and for
the first time we hear the magic word "Persia."[9] He has just time

---

[8] I confess that I do not quite know what to make of her moralizing either
here or in her portrayal of the Persian girl (549ff.). Duckworth (1952), 300-
4, discusses moralizing in Roman comedy but offers no analysis of why it
appears in certain places or certain characters. It is not a stock attribute of the
virgo, but functions here as her chief characteristic.

[9] Here is perhaps as good a place as any to consider Müller's arguments in

enough to praise the costuming (462 *exornatu's basilice*) and check his lead player on his lines. Sagaristio reassures him:

> tragici et comici
> numquam aeque sunt meditati. (465-66)

Tragedians and comedians never knew their lines so well.

A last word on timing (469 *id erit adeundi tempus*), and Toxilus himself is on.

For Dordalus is back (470), full of his own praises for having made money in two ways and in the process having given Attica a

---

favor of a lost expository prologue to the *Persa*, which would have explained both events prior to the play and some that take place within it. One of his minor points is that he believes a prologue is necessary to tell us that Toxilus' master is in Persia, as he has only been said before this to be *peregri* (29-30). Why should we believe the master is in Persia at all? This information comes solely from the mouth and hand of Toxilus, who has every reason to invent such details.

Part of the confusion over this question is due to attempts to date the Greek original of the *Persa* to the period of Middle Comedy on the basis of a line reference (506) to the Persians capturing a town in Arabia. This would seem to presuppose an independent Persia, i.e., before Alexander's conquests. Rather recently Webster (1970), 78-82, contended still that this was a contemporary political reference from the Greek original. Duckworth (1952), 24, and others have shown that the reference is pure fantasy, designed to underline the gullibility of Dordalus. We need no prologue to tell us that the master is in Persia because he is probably nowhere near there.

Müller further asserts a prologue is necessary lest the sale of Sagaristio's daughter seem real and therefore tragic. The audience knows full well from 162-63 that the sale is fictitious. The daughter's apprehensions are real enough, but the audience will no more be fooled by this into thinking the *Persa* a tragedy than is the audience of the *Captivi*. As Halporn pointed out in the talk cited above (n. 4), the comic underplot assures us that the main plot will have a comic resolution, too.

Finally Müller objects to the interrelation of the two money schemes as ambiguous. I argue that the ambiguity is intended (cf. the discussion of the interrelation of the two bets in the *Pseudolus* below). At the play's end, however, there will be no doubt that the credit for success goes to Toxilus and his scheme. By isolating Sagaristio's monologue, Plautus makes this shift possible. The play is perfectly comprehensible without an expository prologue; indeed, such a prologue would sap the improvisatory energy of the play.

new freedwoman. He proclaims how trusting he has been (476 *credebam omnibus*), even talks of reforming himself, and then denies it will ever happen (479). As an audience we might feel some sympathy for Dordalus, knowing he is going to be a victim. Plautus plays on that sympathy, builds it for nine and a half lines—and purges it completely in the half-line in which Dordalus proclaims that he will never change. Toxilus can now remind the audience of the plot he is now setting in motion:

> hunc hominem ego hodie in trasennam doctis deducam dolis,
> itaque huic insidiae paratae sunt probe.   (480-81)

> Today I'll trick this fellow's neck into a noose, so well laid are my snares for him.

The pimp's very first word is to assure Toxilus that he trusts him (482 *credo*). Indeed, he says it so often that he eventually grows quite annoyed with Toxilus, who refuses to respond enthusiastically enough to the pimp's assurances. Dordalus is trying to soothe Tox- ilus' anger at his earlier lack of trust (416) but fails.

Once Toxilus assures himself that his *amica* is free, he opens his trap for Dordalus (493ff.). His speech is full of ironies for the audience to enjoy: Dordalus, he says, will never forget him (494- 95); by doing him this favor, Toxilus is only giving him what he deserves. Toxilus produces the faked letter and refuses to read it himself. Dordalus must. We see just what we shall see in the *Bacchides*: the writer of the letter is a poet/playwright, the man who reads the letter an actor manipulated through his lines. Toxilus even reminds Dordalus to project (500 *clare recitato*). Toxilus promises to be silent during the performance in a richly comic phrase: 500 *hau verbum faciam*. He will not say a word, true, but every word Dordalus will utter is a fiction of Toxilus.

Segal has shown how Plautus plays with forms of *lucrum* (and puns thereon) throughout his characterization of Dordalus.[10] After two formulaic introductory lines of the letter, this multivalent word occurs in emphatic position at the end of the third line (503). And what better symbol could there be to catch the eye of a man as

[10] Segal (1968), 85-87.

obsessed with gain as Dordalus than *Chrysopolis* (506), the city of gold? The exposition grows a bit tedious for Dordalus, and he momentarily threatens to stop reading the letter but is drawn back to it by the power of Fortuna Lucrifera:

> T O X . tace, stultiloque; nescis quid te instet boni
> neque quam tibi Fortuna faculam lucriferam adlucere
> volt.
> D O R . quae istaec lucrifera est Fortuna?   (514-16)

> T O X . Shut up, you windbag. You have no idea of the good around the corner nor how Lady Luck the Loaded wants to shine on you.
> D O R . Who is this Lady Luck the Loaded?

After the reading of the letter, the verbal play with *credo* returns. Since the message was entrusted (528 *creditum*) to a letter, will not Dordalus trust him now (529 *credis*), Toxilus asks? Where is the Persian? Toxilus trusts (530 *credo*) he will soon be there. Toxilus would never have believed (533 *credidi*) Dordalus a coward—and so on. What can be trusted? What is delusion? On this the whole action of the play centers, and it is through his control of the illusion, outside which he stands, that Toxilus will make both the play and Lemniselenis his own.

With the return of Sagaristio and the "Persian girl" (543ff.), the multiple play of fictions becomes dizzying. Ostensibly the form is an eavesdropping scene: Toxilus and Dordalus overhear the conversation of the "Persian" and his captive. Toxilus is in charge of the eavesdropping: note his stage direction at 548: *taciti contemplemus formam*. As the only unselfconscious participant in the scene, however, Dordalus is the real center of the illusion.[11] Outside his illusionistic space stand Sagaristio and the girl, who are part of an

---

[11] We might compare the false Harpax scene in the *Pseudolus* (905-1037). There, though, the victim of the deception is inside the eavesdropping scene. Here Plautus inverts our expectations by putting the victim of the deception on stage as an eavesdropper himself—usually a position of power in such a scene.

illusion, a fiction, a play of which they are in control. Furthest outside stands Toxilus, a ringmaster controlling Dordalus (currently), Sagaristio and the girl (through previous instructions), and the audience (through asides, e.g., 547 *ut contemptim carnufex*, which guides and reinforces audience response to Dordalus).

Toxilus now unites two rings of his circus by hailing Sagaristio (576ff.). He and Dordalus immediately fall to bargaining and seem on the verge of striking a deal, when Toxilus intervenes: he urges Dordalus to question the girl first, before closing the deal (591-92). What can be the dramatic motivation for Toxilus to break off a line of action leading to the conclusion he desires? Only this—his pride as a playwright. Whatever the risks, he cannot forgo the pleasure of manipulating Dordalus and the girl through their scene.[12]

Indeed Dordalus takes a fair amount of prompting. Toxilus must urge him on (600-3) and explain why he (Toxilus) must remain in the background; then in a quick aside he encourages the girl (606-7). After a bustle of introductions and movements, Toxilus feels he must remind her again, only to receive the rather sharp reply that she indeed knows what she is doing (615-16). Toxilus now becomes commentator and interpreter for the audience as she tells her riddling tale. He is now hopeful (622), now fearful (624), now ironically self-assured (629), and finally full of praises for her fine "dramatic ability" (635 *lepide lusit*). Without further comment aside, the scene plays to its conclusion: Dordalus buys the girl and leaves the stage to get the money (672).

In the intermission Toxilus only has time to remind Sagaristio to pretend (677 *simulato*) to leave for the ship and give him a stage direction for doing so (678-79 *per angiportum . . . illac*), before Dordalus returns (683ff.). Dordalus pays for the girl in a gesture that summarizes the interrelation of the two money schemes of the *Persa*. At Sagaristio's request, Dordalus hangs the money pouch around his neck (691-92). The stage picture here, the visual dimension of theatrical meaning, is absolutely vital to our understand-

---

[12] One might compare the scene at the end of the *Miles Gloriosus*, where the slave so convincingly plays grief at leaving the soldier that the *miles* nearly changes his mind, which almost aborts the play (1366-73). In both cases the sheer fun of playing the play carries the performers away from the main issue. The improvisation threatens foreordained design for a moment.

ing of the scene and the play. We see here that the money Sagaristio brought in the pouch around his neck in II.iii has now been replaced, and with ample interest. Sagaristio's money was a help, but it is Toxilus' plot that reaps the impressive success.

Sagaristio now bustles off in great haste, but not before adding one last farcical touch: he is looking for his twin brother (695)! Toxilus thanks him for the prompt (698 *me commonuisti hau male*) and corroborates this wild tale.[13] The "Persian" departs, and Dordalus steps offstage for a moment as well. In this interval the daughter complains that her father is late for his entrance (724 *cessat*). Toxilus hails Saturio (725 *heus, Saturio, exi*), reminds him of his part (724 *admoneam*), and positions him in the wings, ready for his entrance (727 *apscede procul e conspectu*). This second exit of Dordalus is, one must admit, dramatically very ill-motivated—which reminds us of the play as play. He leaves on the vaguest pretext of giving orders to his slaves (722-23), and he returns only to bid Toxilus goodbye—and thank him, after prompting (733-34). The only purpose for his departure is to allow Toxilus to manage the last-minute stage directions noted above. Toxilus can now depart before the storm breaks. Saturio appears to claim his daughter and hauls the pimp off to court (738ff.). We come now to the final scene, a celebration of Toxilus' dramatic triumph (753ff.). Segal's brilliant discussion of this scene as a paradigm of conflict between an agelast (Dordalus) and komastic revellers[14] tends nonetheless to minimize the extent to which Toxilus himself is singled out in the scene. He opens it, flaunting the colors of a military *triumphator*:

hostibu' victis, civibu' salvis, re placida, pacibu' perfectis,
bello extincto, re bene gesta, integro exercitu et praesidiis.

   . . .   (753-54)

The foemen felled,
The city well,
In quiet, peace perfected,

---

[13] All unlooked for, the twin theme reappears. Twins and doubles have an undeniable connection with questions of illusion and reality, though Plautus does not pursue the connection here. Twins are by nature a challenge to the equation of appearance and reality: two different realities have one appearance.
[14] Segal (1968), 87-90.

The war is done
And we have won!
My soldiers, safe collected. . . .

He tells the audience he plans to share his triumph (757), and only then calls the others to the stage. He orders his actors about (758 *ite foras*; 763-64 *agedum | ergo accede ad me atque amplectere sis*) and places them on stage as he wished:

> age, age, age ergo,
> tu Sagaristio, accumbe in summo   (766a-67)

Come, come—come, then, Sagaristio, you take the place of honor.

Dordalus, in contrast to Toxilus' high spirits, enters in the deepest gloom (777ff.). He is extravagant in his grief, and blames it all on the fabrications and machinations of Toxilus. The theatricality of Toxilus' triumph is boldly underscored by Dordalus' recognition line on seeing the assembled revellers: *hoc vide, quae fabulast?* "Look there, what's the story?" (788) The answer is, of course, the play that Toxilus wrote.

The final scene is saturated with the language of the theatre. Compounds of *ludo* are particularly prominent: 771, 803, 805, 811, 833, 843. Dordalus seems to recognize that he is a victim of the power of theatre: he describes Toxilus' victimization of him in "theatrical" verbs: 781 *perfabricavit*; 785 *machinas molitust.*[15] Dordalus calls down curses upon all this theatrical folly:

> qui illum Persam atque omnis Persas atque etiam omnis
>   personas
> male di omnes perdant!   (783-84)

May all the gods damn that Persian and all Persians and all personators!

---

[15] One also wonders if the way Toxilus has twisted Dordalus around (795 *vorsavisti*) has not some relation to the Plautine process of poetic composition (*vortere*).

The verbal chime of *Persas* and *personas* equates the two semantically: the "Persian" who victimized him was an actor.[16] There is even a theatrical threat: if Dordalus does not calm down, they will bring the Persian back (828 *Persam adducam*). On one level, of course, this means that the character could return to do Dordalus further mischief. Dordalus responds to the threat in this sense by accusing Sagaristio of being the Persian (829). Yet I think there is a meta-theatrical undertone to the threat *Persam adducam*. It is also a threat to begin the play again, to repeat the overthrow of Dordalus.[17]

This final scene is very curiously structured. The audience is challenged by two competing play worlds. Formally, this last scene after the entrance of Dordalus resembles an eavesdropping scene. Dordalus stands outside the action of the revellers, observing them. This is no usual eavesdropping scene, however, as Dordalus has no power in the situation despite his initial position. He seems at first to stand outside the stage illusion: 788 *quae fabulast?* This situation is quickly reversed, though, because, once observed, he is treated by the revellers as a spectacle for *their* entertainment. They greet him with applause, for example: 791 *agite, adplaudamus.*

The situation is positively Pirandellian: two competing dramatic worlds cry pretence and reality at one another. In the reconciliatory spirit of comedy an attempt is made to unite these two worlds: the revellers invite Dordalus to pull up a couch and join them for a joint cast party (792 *locus hic tuos est. hic accumbe*), but Dordalus will none of it. The rest of the scene is knockabout farce with Dordalus the butt of all abuse, though just before the end one last attempt is made to invite him to join the revels, this time by Lemniselenis (849 *i intro, amabo*). The two lovers, who most have reason to hate the *leno*, have thus both invited him. He still refuses.

It is impossible to speak of illusion at the end of the *Persa*. We are presented with two competing theatrical modes, two play worlds.

[16] *Persona* originally means mask, and is soon transferred to the character in a play who wears a mask. The more generalized meaning of "person" is much later than Plautus. The *Oxford Latin Dictionary* lists the first examples of this meaning in Cicero.

[17] We must acknowledge that, in the absence of a prologue, there is no proof that the *Persa* was called that by Plautus for his original production. Beare (1963), 170, admits that we cannot tell just how the plays were advertised either. Presumably, a crier would announce the title and author of a play in the absence of a prologue.

The world of Toxilus and his fellow revellers is the world of comedy:
by implication, then, Dordalus' world is the world of tragedy.
Dordalus refuses revelry and refuses comedy. Dordalus was once a
believer in theatrical illusion (recall the wordplay on *credo* above),
but now, having recognized Toxilus' play as a play, he refuses to
give up his own "reality."

We as the audience throw ourselves willingly into the play,
and somewhat surprisingly so does the "author" himself. Toxilus is
firmly inside the play of his own creation in the end, and so a few
further reflections on his character are in order. He is quite unparalleled in Plautus: there is no other *servus amans*. By uniting the
characters of *adulescens* and *servus* in one,[18] Plautus has here united
labor and reward in one character. Where the typical *servus callidus*
labors, and the *adulescens* enjoys the girl in the end, Toxilus does
both. In speaking of the usual Plautine play, the word *hero* is somewhat ambiguous. Formally, the young man seems to be the hero,
since he "gets the girl in the end." Audience sympathy, however,
is likely to rest with the selflessly intriguing slave.[19] In the *Persa*

[18] It is of course impossible to prove that Plautus is in fact responsible. It
is possible that the union was already effected in the Greek archetype. Several
arguments from probability incline me against ascribing the innovation to the
Greek. As Duckworth (1952), 162, notes, the *Persa* takes place among the
lowest strata of Roman society: the pimp, parasite, and daughter are the only
free characters in the play. What we know of New Comedy takes place in quite
a restricted, upper-class world. The slaves and parasites are allowed in only as
hangers-on. Further, slave characters seem to have interested Plautus most. He
would have a good motive for such an essay in character innovation. It must
be admitted that some seams still show in the workmanship: Toxilus' characteristics as lover are on display only in the first and last scenes of the play.
Without this frame the play would be quite typical, with a normal *servus callidus*
role. Finally, I see evidence of Plautine reworking in the interrelation of the
two mechanisms for acquiring money. I would suggest that in the Greek original
a slave, entrusted with money by the *senex* to buy cattle, used this money to
buy the *amica* of the *adulescens*. Then to cover his peculation he devised the
scheme of selling a free girl to the pimp. Plautus has combined the roles of
the *adulescens* and the slave in order to increase the stature of his slave hero
Toxilus. He has reordered events sufficiently to show Toxilus beginning his
own plot before the sudden loan arrives from Sagaristio. By the addition of
the framing first and last scenes, Plautus can make his slave the lover in the
story as well.

[19] See Segal (1968), 164-69, who dispels the notion that the slave is seeking
freedom through his labors. It is not a small point, by the by, that Segal

there is no ambiguity as to who the hero is. Toxilus is virtually the Aristophanic hero reborn.[20]

Nor is there any ambiguity in the hero's own mind. He has the last line of the play (before the one-line epilogue). The line is corrupt, but at least we can say that he is using it to ratify his victory over Dordalus. His last word in that last line (857), functioning like a signature, is his own name.

---

misascribes two lines (263-64) to Toxilus on page 168; they are actually Sagaristio's:

> nunc et amico prosperabo et genio meo multa bona faciam,
> diu quo bene erit, die uno apsolvam: tuxtax tergo erit meo. non curo.

> Now I'll help a friend and do myself a lot of good for the future, too, all in one day. It will be tic-tac-toe on my back—I don't care.

The lines would fit Toxilus perfectly, were he the usual, live-only-for-today, intriguing slave. Toxilus is not, however, even in the center of the play. His eye is on Lemniselenis and the future. This sets him off sharply from the type.

[20] It is therefore superficially plausible when Dumont (1977), 249-60, suggests, on the basis of correspondences in construction, writing, and content, an Aristophanic original for the *Persa*. In light of the fact that Aristophanes did not survive in the repertoire of the hellenistic Artists of Dionysos, the source of most of Plautus' exemplars (see Gratwick [1982], 97), a direct influence seems unfortunately most unlikely.

CHAPTER IV

Six Authors in Search of a Character ~ Asinaria *as Guerrilla Theatre*

THE *Asinaria* is a play full of surprises, of unexpected entrances and exits, of scenes begun in the middle and ended unexpectedly. Despite its modest length, it is a play designed to be played at top speed, so that even a traditional scene like the deception of the ass-dealer is crowded off the stage in the rush. The rush is so great, in fact, that we may be left only with memories of an unruly gabble of voices when the play is done. What, if anything, holds the play together?

Traditional analyst criticism of the play would have it that nothing does. It has sought to separate the play into at least two elements, which are then said to derive from two Greek originals, which Plautus has contaminated to produce the *Asinaria*.[1] This process has not been without effort: even Hough, anxious to find evidence of contamination, grudgingly admits that the *Asinaria* "does not at first sight present [a] mass of contradictions."[2] I will argue here that the *Asinaria* is indeed unified, and that the unifying element is the conflict of various would-be authors or *poetae* who successively seize or attempt to seize control of the play's plot.[3]

The *Asinaria* possesses a typically metatheatrical Plautine prologue. One might be inclined to ask what prologues are *not* meta-

---

[1] The most convenient and succinct discussion of contamination in Roman comedy is to be found in Beare (1963), 310-13. For analyst views of the play, see Hough (1937), 19-37, and della Corte (1951), 289-306. For a survey of views of the play, see Bertini's edition (1968), 48-59.

[2] Hough (1937), 19.

[3] Another interesting and valuable defense of the unity of the play is provided by Konstan (1978), 215-21. See also Konstan (1983), 47-56. He sees the play as a conservative moral critique of materialism; this then is the thread that holds together the shifting plot paradigms of the play (which he types as the ethical, the rival, and a blend of the two). He outlines major shifts in the plot, but I see the shifts as more frequent and pervasive. Nor can I share his relatively positive view of the play's resolution (see below, n. 8).

theatrical. The surprising answer for ancient drama would seem to be most of them. Our scanty evidence suggests that the Menandrean prologue spoke from within the world of the play, to judge from Pan in the *Dyskolos*. The god shares the knowledge he has by virtue of his divinity with the audience, but he never steps out of character in doing so.[4] The Terentian prologue by contrast stands totally outside the play that follows. These prologues are advertisements for the play that follows, with not even a hint of illusory playing. They sometimes speak with the voice of the producer, sometimes with that of the author, but the *prologus* never acknowledges his own role as *actor*. Unlike the Menandrean or Terentian *prologus*, the anonymous Plautine speaker can speak both from within and from without the world of his play. The *prologus* of the *Asinaria* acknowledges his role as actor even as he draws the audience into his own world:

> Hoc agite sultis, spectatores, nunciam,
> quae quidem mihi atque vobis res vortat bene
> gregique huic at dominis atque conductoribus.   (1-3)

> Step this way now, if you please, spectators, which will do
> both me and you good—and this acting company and our
> managers and producers.

He is furthermore a self-conscious player: he manages to comment on both his past and future statements *as lines*: i.e., for a moment only he steps out of his written lines, it seems, to reassure the audience that the plot is no great problem, then by a seemingly clumsy periphrasis pulls himself back to his appointed course:

> nam quod ad argumentum attinet, sane brevest.
> nunc quod me dixi velle vobis dicere
> dicam: huic nomen graece Onagost fabulae;   (8-10)

> As for the plot, it's short enough. Now what I told you I

---

[4] Cf. the Lar who speaks the prologue of the *Aulularia*; not all Plautine prologues are metatheatrical. See the discussion of prologues in Chapter VIII below.

wanted to tell you I'll tell you—in Greek this play is called the *Onagos*.

With the first scene we already see two authors at work: Demaenetus and his slave Libanus. The moment these two actors enter, their masks tell us what to expect in general from the scene: we have a *senex* and a *servus callidus*. We naturally expect the clever slave to launch an intrigue against his master at any moment. The slave is ready to ask his master a question (what question, interestingly enough, we never find out). Suddenly Demaenetus the *senex* wrenches control of the scene away from Libanus by showing that he already knows of his son's love affair; not only that, he refuses to play the usual father's role in this situation that the play and Libanus would like to assign him:

> DE. . . . qur hoc ego ex te quaeram? aut qur miniter tibi
> propterea quod me non scientem feceris?
> aut qur postremo filio suscenseam,
> patres ut faciunt ceteri?
> LI.   quid istuc novi est?   (47-50)

> DE. Why should I question you? Why threaten you,
> because you didn't inform me? Why for that matter should I
> get mad at my own son, as other fathers do?
> LI. What novelty is this?

Quid istuc novi indeed: Demaenetus seems bent on rewriting the course of the typical Roman comedy. Libanus is somewhat shocked by this sudden turn of events, but recovers gamely in three lines and prepares to play second banana for a while (50-54). Demaenetus remains in charge until the end of the scene. We soon discover, too, that the theatre is in his blood, for his own father not only was similarly a playwright in the young Demaenetus' love affair but even took a part in the play he had written by dressing up as a *nauclericus* to swindle a slave-dealer out of a girl for Demaenetus:

> volo me patris mei similem, qui caussa mea
> nauclerico ipse ornatu per fallaciam
> quam amabam abduxit ab lenone mulierem;   (68-70)

I want to imitate my father: for my sake he swindled the girl
I loved from her owner by dressing up as a ship's captain.

When we learn that he has lost the father's role to his wife,
however, we suspect that he will not be any more successful in
keeping control of this play than he has been in keeping control of
his marriage (78-79).

The play Demaenetus wishes to write turns out to be quite
simple and banal: he wishes his slave to cheat him (Demaenetus)
out of the money needed for the son's amours (91). Not only that:
he even needs a ghostwriter for this very simple play, for he must
leave the details of the plot to the slave Libanus (96), who now,
albeit on another's terms, regains control of the scene. The moment
of innovation passes. The plot will remain much the same as in a
typical Roman comedy; only the self-consciousness of the participants
marks this play off, for Demaenetus knows what is going on, and
Libanus knows that he knows. Libanus gets the strong exit (117),
while Demaenetus is left trailing weakly behind.

Two more authors, one after the other, now appear on the
scene: Demaenetus' son, Argyrippus, and the *lena*, Cleareta, mother
of Argyrippus' mistress. The plays they wish to write are none too
surprising: Argyrippus would have the lady of his love without
excessive expense or inconvenience and vainly threatens to turn the
play into a tragedy unless he gets his way:

> ego pol te redigam eodem unde orta es, ad egestatis
> terminos,
> ego edepol te faciam ut quae sis nunc et quae fueris scias.
> quae priu' quam istam adii atque amans ego animum meum
> isti dedi,
> sordido vitam oblectabas pane in pannis inopia,
> atque ea si erant, magnas habebas omnibus dis gratias;
> eadem nunc, quom est melius, me quoius opera est ignoras
> mala.
> reddam ego te ex fera fame mansuetem, me specta modo.

(139-45)

Darn it, I'll send you right back to the poorhouse, where

you started from. I'll make you realize what you are—and what you *were*. Before I approached that girl and like a lover gave her my heart, you scraped along on scraps, wearing rags, in poverty—and thanked all the gods that you had *that* much. Now when times are better, you snub me, the founder of the feast. I'll tame your temper with starvation, just watch me.

Meanwhile, the *lena* is content to perform her part just as it is usually depicted in the arts—and says as much!

> quid me accusas, si facio officium meum?
> nam neque fictum usquamst neque pictum neque scriptum in
>   poematis
> ubi lena bene agat cum quiquam amante quae frugi esse volt.
>
> (173-75)

Why blame me for doing my bit? Nowhere in fiction, pictures, or scripts has any madam worth her salt treated a lover well.

Line 173 is perhaps the best evidence for the technical use of *officium* as "role" or "stock part in a play." Though in other circumstances it might be translated "duty," here the lena's *officium* is set in apposition to literary and artistic representations. She also insists on the young man's keeping to his usual role:

> is dare volt, is se aliquid posci, nam ibi de pleno promitur;
> neque ille scit quid det, quid damni faciat: illi rei studet.
>
> (181-82)

[The new lover] wants to give, to be asked for things—he pays from a full purse. He doesn't know what he gives, what it costs. He's eager in the matter.

Indeed this whole scene would be stale and hackneyed in the extreme were it not for the fact of the games-playing self-consciousness of the participants. The *lena* uses her "literary" knowledge to wound with irony. The young lover is caught in the metatheatrical dilemma: conscious that he is playing a role, but unable to seize control of his own play and destiny. Beneath these "seeming" roles and the reality of the pain we sense the familiar contrast of *logos* and *ergon*, once made explicit as *lingua* and *factis* (162).

These two yield the stage, without any noticeable progress having been made, to the current onlie begetter of the drama, Libanus. He, however, is suffering from writer's block: despite considerable mental exertion on his part, no ideas seem to be coming (249-64). He also seems confused by the unusual role he must now play in cooperating with, not deceiving, his master:

> serva erum, cave tu idem faxis alii quod servi solent,
> qui ad eri fraudationem callidum ingenium gerunt. (256-57)

> Take care of your master, don't do as other slaves do, who
> put their wits to fleecing the master.

He is only saved by another hoary theatrical device, the *servus ex machina* in the form of his fellow slave Leonida, who comes running in (265).

It is now that Libanus conclusively loses control of the play to a ghostwriter. Despite two later imperatives (367) and a sarcastic reminder to Leonida of his "real" part in the play (i.e., the outer play, not the plot they are constructing) in a parting shot,

> quin tuom officium facis ergo ac fugis? (380)

> Why don't you act your part—and escape?

Libanus can no longer claim to be in charge. He has proved to be just as helpless as Demaenetus. Despite his surface claims to authority, his real loss of power is underlined by the foreshadowing of the coming slapstick, where he will be the physical butt:

> LE. pugno malam si tibi percussero,
>   mox quom Sauream imitabor, caveto ne suscenseas.
>   (371-72)

If I land a punch on your jaw while I'm imitating Saurea,
don't you get irritated.

Compare:

LE. . . . em ergo hoc tibi.
LI.   hospes, te opsecro, defende. (431)

LE. There, take that!
LI. Sir, I beg you, save me!

The scene that follows, while on the surface a typical
deception scene with the ass-dealer pitted against Leonida and Libanus, is portrayed as strictly improvised throughout. The only
element of the scene we know in advance is that Leonida will play
the part of the steward Saurea—but he has already improvised that
role in a previous offstage scene (which we learned in 352). The
details of the deception have not been worked out in advance, and
indeed they must here and there be adjusted to audience response.
Libanus greets the ass-dealer and corroborates the description of
"Saurea" as Leonida has already played him. Then Leonida blusters
in, playing to the hilt the role of angry overseer. At one point Leonida
is getting carried away with this role, upstaging the other two, and
must be pulled back to the real purpose of the scene, the deception,
by the less engaged Libanus:

heus jam satis tu.
audin quae loquitur?   (446-47)

Hey, enough of that. Do you hear what he says?

Libanus, even if he is not equal to designing the overall plot, shows
himself to be an excellent improvisational actor by playing a double
role within the scene: angry in the first half of a line with the trader
to oblige the angry "Saurea," and pleading, seeking sympathy, in
an aside to the same trader in the second half of the line:

flagitium hominis. da, opsecro, argentum huic, ne male
                    loquatur.   (473)

You walking felony! (Please, give him the money, so
the curses will stop.)

Leonida's sudden and rather curious change of tone at 496 (from
angry to conciliatory), often pointed to as proof of contamination or
radical reworking of the original of the scene because of its seeming
emotional inexplicability in the context of the preceding angry scene,
is in fact yet another mark of improvisation. It is the beginning of
a new tack which does not work. I do not believe it has been noted
before that the ass-dealer is inconsistent in his role as well. Whereas
before Leonida in the guise of Saurea arrives on the scene, the trader
expressly states that, had Saurea been there, he would have handed
over the money, the arrival of the quite convincingly played "Saurea"
seems rather to harden his resistance to any such manoeuvre (396;
cf. 455-56). The connecting theme in the *Asinaria* may be the failure
of all the successive playwrights who try to control the play.

The *lena* is having problems with her own play, too, as the
following scene shows (504-44), for her daughter has been so in-
judicious as to fall in love with Argyrippus and now refuses to play
as heartless a role as her mercenary mother would assign her.

Gloom and failure seem banished with the slaves' return, however (545). With the aid of the old man the plot has succeeded.
Indeed, the slaves, after celebrating their own skills, seem properly
appreciative of Demaenetus' histrionic accomplishments:

edepol senem Demaenetum lepidum fuisse nobis:
ut adsimulabat Sauream med esse quam facete!   (580-81)

Old Demaenetus was a real sport to us. Look how sharply he
pretended I was Saurea.

Libanus claims the first place for himself by opening the scene, and
Leonida temporarily defers to him in the high spirits of the moment,
but we soon learn that it is Leonida who actually has the money in
his possession (579) and therefore now possesses the real power and
control.[5]

[5] Not surprisingly, this too has been taken as evidence for contamination.
How, the analyst asks, should Libanus *not* know his fellow slave has the money?

When Argyrippus and Philaenium now arrive on the scene, they bring with them the rhetoric of tragedy. The tearful parting of these two lovers threatens to turn comedy on its head—but the eavesdroppers prevent this. Libanus and Leonida have remained on stage, not only to entertain the audience with asides (e.g, 598-605), but by their mocking presence as spectators of the scene to assure us we are still watching a comedy.

The play could easily end here; the slaves need only turn over the money, and all may live happily ever after. Flushed with their recent success, however, the two slaves are tempted to an encore. Thus ensues the curious scene of games-playing for its own sake,[6] in which the master must supplicate first Leonida, then Libanus, for his money. The two slaves manipulate Argyrippus and Philaenium throughout the scene, giving them stage directions and forcing them to accept suppliant roles quite out of their usual characters. The scene ends in boisterous slapstick, as Libanus rides horseback on his master Argyrippus. The tragic tone is banished by triumphantly theatrical (visual) demonstration. Note the order: the weaker and provenly unsuccessful Libanus is given primacy of place; he even claims to be a god(-ess), Salvation (713). We are meant, I believe, to doubt that the salvation he arranges is likely to be a lasting one. There are two other ominous undercurrents: the first mention of Argyrippus' rival for Philaenium, Diabolus (634), and the sudden conditionality of the father's help in that he now demands a night with the girl as the price of that help (736). Demaenetus' success with his first playwriting effort seems to have gone to his head, for the *senex* has now written a vehicle for himself to star in. The shadow of the mother, however, hangs over his new venture:

> LE. . . . ne uxor resciscat metuit.
>   de argento si mater tua sciat ut sit factum—   (743-44)

He's afraid of his wife finding out. If your mother knew how the money was got . . .

Well, for one thing the question is merely a "feed" line, designed for the audience's information, not Libanus', and for another it underscores the irony of Libanus' boasts compared to his real lack of control.

[6] Note all the *ludo* compounds in the scene: 677, 679, 711, 730, 731.

Our last authors are about to arrive: Diabolus, the rival of Argyrippus, and his parasite. Diabolus is a typical *adulescens* in that he,
too, is incapable of plotting in his own behalf to acquire Philaenium.
The playwright of his play is actually the parasite:

nam tu poeta es prosus ad eam rem unicus. (748)

For you're the one and only poet for this affair.

Like Shaw, the parasite writes far too many stage directions into his
play, so we know immediately that he is unlikely to see a performance
that will satisfy him. His comic list of restrictions of Philaenium's
conduct show the parasite and Diabolus to be as much the enemies
of *ludus* as any agelastic *senex*. Note that Diabolus is also afraid of
the power of other poet/artists. He particularly fears writing and
painting:

aut quod illa dicat peregre allatam epistulam,
ne epistula quidem ulla sit in aedibus
nec cerata adeo tabula; et si qua inutilis
pictura sit, eam vendat. . . . (761-64)

As for her saying she has a letter from abroad, she's not to
have a single letter in the house, or even stationery. And if
she has any unsuitable painting, let her sell it.

Like moral reformers throughout the ages, Diabolus fears the power
of art to shape the life of the viewer. An improper letter or painting
could give Philaenium ideas—and no playwright of Diabolus' sort
likes letting his characters have their own ideas. The parasite's elaborate script comes to grief quite soon (811ff.), when Diabolus learns
that his rival is before him with the necessary money. Diabolus
himself comes up with the idea that sparks the next play (to tell
Demaenetus' wife, line 811), but the writing must be left to the
parasite (820-27).

Demaenetus' starring vehicle, meanwhile, is progressing to his
complete satisfaction, if not to his son's. Indeed, he begins to enjoy
the role a bit too much, to go too far with it. The price of his help,

one night with Philaenium, is proving a bitter experience for his son Argyrippus:[7]

> DE. unum hunc diem perpetere, quoniam tibi potestatem
>   dedi
>   cum hac annum ut esses, atque amanti argenti feci
>   copiam.
> ARG. em istoc me facto tibi devinxti.
> DE. quin te ergo hilarum das mihi?   (847-50)

> DE. Just put up with this one day, since I've given you a
> year's lease on the girl and put money in the lover's, too.
> ARG. Yes, you've conquered me with that stroke.
> DE. Then why don't you put a smile on for me?

Just as Argyrippus is forced to this painful and humiliating surrender, leaving him far from *hilarum*, Artemona, wife of Demaenetus, and the parasite arrive as unnoticed eavesdroppers on this scene. Once again, their presence and the promise of slapstick comedy embodied in Artemona's *matrona* mask rescue for comedy a scene that has veered dangerously near the tragic.

The audience now awaits knowingly for the storm to break. Demaenetus declares himself ready to become another Menaechmus:

> DE. egon ut non domo uxori meae
>   surrupiam in deliciis pallam quam habet atque ad te
>   deferam,
>   non edepol conduci possum vita uxoris annua. (884-86)

> DE. Why don't I steal from home my wife's favorite cloak

---

[7] Demaenetus forfeits some of the sympathy he gained by his earlier understanding attitude. Demaenetus' father, who played a *nauclericus* to help out in his son's love affair, evidently did so without seeking a reward. Demaenetus does not follow his father's good example. There is a flavor of tragedy here, which may be an intentional but subtle echo. Argyrippus is asked to endure only one day of cuckoldry. We might compare Odysseus' request of Neoptolemos in the *Philoctetes* to give up his scruples for "one brief, shameless portion of a day" (Sophocles *Philoctetes* 83). See also Konstan (1978), 216.

and give it to you? I couldn't be hired *not* to, even if my
wife dropped dead within the year.

Compare

hanc modo uxori intus pallam surrupui, ad scortum fero.
(Menaechmi 130)

I stole this cloak from my wife now; I'm taking it to my
girlfriend.

His expression of this sentiment is his downfall, for it is overheard
by Artemona. When he demands applause for his performance a
few lines later,

pueri, plaudite et mi ob jactum cantharo mulsum date. (906)

Give me a cheer, boys, and a drink, in honor of that throw.

we know he is likely to fare no better than any of the other failed
playwrights we have seen in the course of the *Asinaria*.
The final playwright arrives like an avenging fury, scattering
all other designs before her. Artemona catches her husband in a very
compromising situation and hauls him away to justice. Yet is she
finally any more successful than the other playwrights? She has her
husband back, but he is no great prize. In the final confusion, her
son slips away with the girl (941), and a happy ending to Argyrippus'
play might at least seem to be in the offing.
The parting lines of the parasite of Diabolus cast this into doubt,
though:

poste demum huc cras adducam ad lenam, ut viginti minas
ei det, in partem hac amanti ut liceat ei potirier.
Argyrippus exorari spero poterit ut sinat
sese alternas cum illo noctes hac frui. (915-18)

Afterwards, tomorrow, I'll bring [Diabolus] here, to pay
the madam 80 minae for a partial share in the girl. I do

hope Argyrippus can be persuaded to let my master share
her alternate nights.

The parasite has remained outside the action, in the eavesdropper's
position. He stands in closer communication with the audience than
do the other players at this point, and by his position he should have
our sympathies. His proposal for a time-sharing arrangement between his master Diabolus and Argyrippus is therefore disturbing.
Will this scheme be adopted and Argyrippus' happiness undercut
thereby? We do not learn from this play.

It does not seem unreasonable, then, to call the *Asinaria* a tale
of failed improvisation, for no one gets what he wants in full.
Argyrippus and Diabolus may, with Solomonic justice, each have
half a girl. The girl, Philaenium, who protested her love for Argyrippus alone, may have to endure Diabolus as well. The slaves
Libanus and Leonida did have their fun, but their schemes never
quite worked as planned. Demaenetus was never the success at playwriting he aspired to be, either as friend to his son, or as self-
interested old lecher. Artemona has her husband back, for what he
is worth, but her son has escaped her control.[8]

The action is not over with the final exits of these characters—
nor is the play. A short epilogue remains (942-47), building a picture
frame around the action, even though some of the action slips behind
the frame or behind the visible background. The epilogue was
probably not unique to Plautus, though Terence never has more

[8] Konstan (1978), 221, finds in this ending a reaffirmation of values: "The
Asinaria is thus more than a clever variation on comic paradigms; it is also a
defense of the ethical structure of the ancient patriarchal family against the
corruption of money and passion, and reflects the profound moral conservatism
of the author."

Konstan (1983) is virtually a reprint of Konstan (1978) with the addition
of a few footnotes. He still argues that the ending restores Demaenetus to his
position as *paterfamilias* and the family to a state of harmony: Konstan (1978)
217 equals Konstan (1983) 31. As long as Diabolus and Argyrippus are sharing
the girl, though, the restoration of family, values, and moral order is still to
my mind deeply ambiguous. As John Wright (1982), 507, has said of this
play: "Without exception, the characters are as unsympathetic as their actions
are unedifying. . . . If there is any unifying theme to the play, this theme is
sadism, with one character after another alternatively playing the role of torturer
and victim."

than a quick farewell and an injunction to applause and no fragment from an epilogue can be securely identified in the remains of the other early writers of Roman comedy. Unique or not, the epilogue stands with one foot in the world of the play and one foot in the world of the spectators. A mediator is needed between the two worlds, and as the prologue led us in, so the epilogue leads us out again. The world of Plautus' plays is by no means a naturalistic one. It is a world of games-playing where rules quite different from those of life obtain.

Yet there is communication between these two worlds. The audience is assured that it can save old Demaenetus from a beating— by loud applause:

> nunc si voltis deprecari huic seni ne vapulet,
> remur impetrari posse, plausum si clarum datis. (946-47)

> Now if you want to save this old man from a beating, we think you can, if you applaud loud enough.

The audience is thus an essential participant in the play. Its response will determine old Demaenetus' fate.[9]

Power in the *Asinaria* resides with those who watch, and the ultimate watchers, the furthest circle out, are the audience. The *Asinaria* is not an emotionally satisfactory play: it is a play about repeated failures of improvisation. These improvisations fail because, ultimately, someone is watching from the outside. Vigilant morality, in the form of the *matrona*, has seen all and finally moves in to end the *ludi*.

Is there no hope, then, for the spirit of revelry and holiday? Only a little—it is the hope offered by the epilogue, the power of applause to save the *senex*. It would be idle to speculate whether some particular pressure (whether from the state or the festival producer) had been exerted on Plautus to write a moral play, showing

---

[9] The end of the *Cistellaria* (782-87) shows the more immediate effects of audience response to a performance. Those who have succeeded in their roles get a drink, those who have failed, a beating. In the epilogue to the *Captivi*, there is a more general appeal for applause in order that virtue may be rewarded (1029ff.).

virtue triumphant—such pressures were always present in Roman society. The audience has seen the *matrona* undo the holiday spirit of the end of the *Asinaria*. With the final lines, though, the spectators are offered the chance to undo her action. Through the thunder of applause Plautine comedy can be reborn and the comic cycle renewed.[10]

[10] As Tinkerbell is revived by the audience's applause in J. M. Barrie's *Peter Pan?*

CHAPTER V

The Pilots of Penance ～ or ～
The Slave of Lust

THE *Casina* is at the same time one of the most lively and most curious plays in the Plautine corpus. Its virtues are in part its very departure from, or omission of, standard Roman comedy plot elements. We must confront some of its curiosities before we can appreciate those virtues.

With the very first few lines of the prologue of the *Casina*, we are plunged into a problem scholars have found nearly as bedevilling as that of the Greek original: the problem of interpolation and redaction. To what extent can we be sure the text of the play as it has been transmitted to us is identical with the one that left Plautus' hand?

In the prologue to the *Casina* we are confronted with irrefutable evidence that this part of the play at least has been altered for a revival performance. Lines 5ff. refer to the success the play had in its first performance, and justify, by the pleasant metaphor of old wine, the decision to revive it now:[1]

> qui utuntur vino vetere sapientis puto
> et qui lubenter veteres spectant fabulas. . . .   (5-6)

I think that those who appreciate old wine and old plays are equally wise.

---

[1] I say lines 5ff. advisedly, because the extent of interpolation and redaction remains open to debate. MacCary and Willcock in their recent and valuable edition of the play hew a conservative line in assigning only lines 5-22 to the revival performance: MacCary and Willcock (1976), 97. In this they follow K. Abel (1955), 55-61, and Leo (1912), 207 n. 2, who opted for 5-20. Yet it is by no means certain that the topical references to military success (1-4), financial difficulties (23-28), and Apulia as Roman territory (72) belong to the original prologue: see Frank (1933), 368.

Before we go on to consider the play itself, let us first account for some of the peculiarities of the prologue.

The prologue and epilogue, as we have seen elsewhere (cf. the discussion of the *Asinaria* above), form a frame around the stage action; yet how different is the spirit of this prologue from that in the *Asinaria*. There is no play with the duality of the position of the *prologus* within and without the play. The *Asinaria* prologue provides transition from the outer world, an induction into the world of the play. The prologue of the *Casina* stands outside the play entirely. He emphasizes that the players are merely a troupe of actors:[2]

> benigne ut operam detis ad nostrum gregem. (22)

> Kindly give your attention to our company.

He banters with the audience; in 75 he offers to bet with them on the truth of one of his assertions. Like a preacher asking for an amen, he demands applause at the very beginning to be sure he has the audience's approval and attention:

> si verum dixi, signum clarum date mihi. . . . (3)

> If I've spoken the truth, give me a loud sign of it.

None of this, however, initiates any movement into the world of the play.

The suggestion first made by Skutsch that the speaker is Fides is no solution to the problem of the nature of this curious prologue.[3] On the analogy of Pan in Menander's *Dyskolos*, Fides should speak from within the play, not from the outside like a Terentian prologue.

---

[2] He also refers in 83 to the *comoedia* they are about to perform. He even makes an obscene joke (84-86) about the price of the supposedly chaste heroine's virtue after the play is over. There is a curious irony to this reference, which Forehand (1973), 255 n. 11, quite misses with his suggestion of a homosexual reference (i.e., that the heroine after the play is just a male actor): there *is* no heroine, onstage or off. The audience, experiencing the play linearly, of course does not yet know that the joke is built around an empty core, but it is still puzzling.

[3] Skutsch (1914), 272-85.

One might compare Euclio's Lar, who speaks the prologue in the *Aulularia* (1-39). In three other Plautine prologues (*Amphitruo, Rudens,* and *Trinummus*) the deities who speak them play now inside, now outside the world of the play (though more of the former). We have no trace of such Plautine gamesmanship in the prologue of the *Casina*.

No other prologue gives us so much irrelevant information about the Greek original. We learn from the prologue that Casina has a typical New Comedy personal history: exposed at birth, found by a slave of Lysidamus' household, and brought up by Cleostrata virtually as a daughter (37-46). The old slave is now lying sick in the house (37-38), which is apparently meant to account for his absence from the play, though in fact we do not know from the prologue that he will never appear. Of what relevance is this slave at all? The natural assumption is that he played a key role in the recognition scene, which established Casina as a freeborn citizen and therefore eligible to wed young Euthynicus. Yet all we have of such a scene is a two-line summary in the epilogue (1013-14). We will never see any of the three characters most central to the action, at least of the underlying Diphilean play: Casina, her young lover Euthynicus, and the slave who makes the recognition possible.

The prologue and epilogue to the *Casina* do not explicate, they supplement. Moreover, they are not a necessary supplement. The action of the *Casina* is perfectly intelligible without them. Why the great divorce?

It is clear that Plautus has simply excised great chunks of the Diphilean plot from his treatment. K. Abel suggested that he suppressed the entire love and recognition plot because his audience had by now become bored with this New Comedy staple.[4] If so, why does he put that same dull material, almost duller in schematic outline than it would be in action, back into the prologue? There is not the slightest clue in the prologue that all the events of Casina's story, if not that of her lover, will not in fact be represented. If Plautus' audience *were* by now sated with this sort of thing, they would quite likely on the basis of this prologue get up and leave for the bear-baiting show.[5] On the other hand, if the audience were still interested

[4] K. Abel (1955), 59.
[5] Terence's first audience for the *Hecyra* deserted the play in favor of a rope-dancer, as the prologue to that play tells us.

in such plots, they would certainly have been confused, even angry, at finding none of this material in the play. In either instance, it is a case of false advertising: in the latter case intentionally deceptive, in the former merely botched, and smacking of a pedantry quite alien to Plautus.

Pedantry—we may have a clue here. K. Abel remarks that Plautus here describes his own activity not with the usual verb *vortere*, but with the unusual *scribere*.[6] H. D. Jocelyn, in an article on the prologue of the *Poenulus*, notes that explicit references to the poet's name are infrequent among the preserved eighteen prologues of Plautus and are likely to be a sign of late interpolation.[7] They occur three times, once adjectivally, in the *Casina* prologue: 12, 34,[8] and 65. Jocelyn also offers the interesting suggestion that some of the detailed information about the Greek original of the *Poenulus* may have been a scholar's interpolation into the prologue at a time of revival of interest in early Latin plays.[9] He confines this suggestion to a few lines giving little more information than the name of the Greek original.

Something similar may have happened, on a much larger scale, to the prologue of the *Casina*. The whole of 30-83 seems to reflect someone's interest in filling in all that Plautus left out. It is perhaps most economical to assume only one revision of the prologue. If so, that revision was almost total: lines 5-22 and 30-83 certainly are post-Plautine; the topical references in 1-4 and 23-39 are at home in either period, as is the banter in 84-88. If anything belongs with certainty to the original prologue, it is not apparent.

What motive can we assign for the revision? Our answer must necessarily be speculative. Perhaps the period of scholarly interest to which Jocelyn refers began about the time of the *Casina* revival. More likely, tastes and standards may have been changing steadily since Plautus' death. We know that Terence felt it necessary to defend himself against charges of serious departures from his originals.[10]

---

[6] K. Abel (1955), 59. His explanation is that Plautus, having altered his original so radically, uses this term to denote an equality with the original author that he now feels entitled to claim.

[7] Jocelyn (1969), 119-20.

[8] Where the curious expansion *cum latranti nomine* is added. Is this an exceedingly feeble joke or an attempt to jog the audience's memory?

[9] Jocelyn (1969), 119-20.

[10] E.g., the prologues to the *Eunuch* and *Andria*.

The seams, if any, in the prologue would not be perceptible to an audience on first hearing.

THE PLAY proper opens abruptly in a scene of lively quarrelling (89-143) between the two slave rivals for the hand of Casina: Olympio, the farm overseer, and Chalinus, personal slave of the absent young master Euthynicus. As spectators we are plunged immediately into the central controversy of the play: the theme of sexual rivalry. The humor of the scene lies in the strutting-cock image Olympio projects of himself, an image we will eventually see shattered. There is no hint in the text of the scene itself that either slave sees himself as a surrogate for one of the masters, young or old. Olympio's vision of sexual bliss with Casina, combined with the discomfiture of his rival Chalinus (132-40), is explicit and uncompromising.[11]

The next scene opens with the appearance of Cleostrata (144) and her opening soliloquy (148-64). From this we learn that she sides with her son and against her husband in the contest over Casina. An analyst critic might take exception to a phrase she uses in 151: her husband Lysidamus opposes both her and her son in this matter out of willfulness *amorisque causa sui*. This implies that Cleostrata already knows of her husband's designs on Casina; she also charges him with just this in a statement to her neighbor Myrrhina:

sed ipsus eam amat.   (1959)

But he himself loves her.

Yet a good deal later in the play (531) she will come storming out in angry surprise at just this same piece of information, which she seems to learn for certain only via Chalinus' eavesdropping in 470.

[11] MacCary and Willcock (1976), 111, rightly compare the scene between Tranio and Grumio with its similar city/country rivalry that opens the *Mostellaria*. Forehand (1973), 237-38, sees a uniquely intense bitterness in the Olympio/Chalinus scene. One might note that there is a good deal of bitterness between Tranio and Grumio, whose source of contention (the present young master's pleasure versus the distant old master's wrath) is much less serious and personal. This scene functions as a prologue to the *Mostellaria*. The Olympio/Chalinus scene, introducing all necessary elements of the *Casina*, could equally well function as the prologue of *its* play. Perhaps the original production of the *Casina* had no prologue.

What are we to think? Has Plautus pulled this soliloquy out of a later position in the original Greek play and put it here, failing as he converts the speech into a *canticum* to excise this piece of information which Cleostrata should not yet have? Or has he carelessly slipped it in on his own? Neither, I think.[12]

The soliloquy is a step outside the action of the play. It is often viewed as the awkward substitute for the inner monologue or omniscient narrator of prose narrative. It is *not* that, but something much more interesting and useful. As J. L. Styan puts it: "The fundamental purpose of the aside or soliloquy is to engage the spectator directly, to throw him a face-to-face challenge to agree or disagree: they are a reminder to all that a play is in progress."[13] The function of Cleostrata's soliloquy here is exactly this: Plautus is already demanding that we choose sides, and he wants to make it clear that, somewhat atypically for Roman comedy, the side to choose is that of the *matrona*. She is taking the absent son's part, of course, and with him we naturally sympathize. With her we need more reason to sympathize, and the dramatically anachronistic knowledge of her husband's illicit passion supplies that motivation for us.

As an audience we need such firm orientation to guide us through the next few scenes, beginning with the one between the wife Cleostrata and Myrrhina, her neighbor (165-216). Cleostrata could easily lose our sympathy here by seeming to be the typical scolding wife. Myrrhina speaks with the sweet voice of reason and tolerance: let Lysidamus have his fun. What does it matter if he chases after young girls, so long as he keeps his wife in comfort at home (206-7)? Against the spirit of comedy and fun that Myrrhina presents, Cleostrata could easily be made out an agelastic villainess.[14]

---

[12] One must consider a third possibility. Does Cleostrata in fact know all along? If so, we must supply a good bit of the story on our own. How she found out must remain a mystery. Furthermore, in the spirit of not telling family secrets before servants, she does not disclose what might tactically be a very valuable piece of information—that Lysidamus is the real rival—to her only effective ally in the play, the slave Chalinus. Her motive then for the outburst of 531ff. must be the fact that Lysidamus in his haste has set up his assignation with Casina within the hour and right under his wife's nose in the neighbor's house. This weakens the impact of her decision finally to do something about her husband's philandering.

[13] Styan (1975), 153.

[14] Forehand applies the term *blocking* to her. But she is not the typical Plautine

Instead Plautus has already begun a process of reorienting our perceptions of, and reactions to, the stock types in the *Casina*.[15] Cleostrata is not merely an agelastic *matrona*, standing in the way of her husband's good, dirty fun. She is a sympathetic but not submissive woman, sexually under attack by her husband's philandering, a rejection made doubly cruel by his quasi-incestuous designs on a girl she has raised like a daughter (46; 194). Unlike virtually every other *matrona* in Roman comedy, she will do something more than complain about it.

The dialogue of the two *matronae* is put to an end by the appearance of Lysidamus. His soliloquy also invites the audience to agree or disagree. MacCary and Willcock have noted the persistent pattern in the play whereby food and sex are, not surprisingly, associated.[16] Plautus does more than associate the two, I think. Here some have seen Lysidamus take on the role of the *adulescens amans*.[17] But has he truly become rejuvenated like an Aristophanic hero? Could he, like the young, live on love? No, love is not *food* to him— it is a spice.[18]

nam ubi amor condimentum inerit, quoivis placituram
⟨escam⟩ credo;
neque salsum neque suave esse potest quicquam, ubi amor
non admiscetur. . . .   (221-22)

Now when love is the spice, I think the meal will please

---

blocking character or agelast. Segal (1968), 28-29, cites the *Casina* for the natural husband/wife antagonism of Roman comedy, but in his discussion of agelasts (70-98) he does not include the *matrona* with the *leno* and the *miles* as implacable enemies of comic freedom. Despite all the jokes against the *matrona*, there is a grudging respect for married love in Plautus.

[15] Forehand in his *Arethusa* article contends that Plautus plays unusual variations on stock types and themes in the *Casina*. I intend to go further and argue below that these variations fall within a frame of inversions and transformations that are transferrals of characteristics among these types.

[16] MacCary and Willcock (1976), 32ff. See also MacCary (1974).

[17] E.g., Forehand (1973), 239.

[18] Casina herself is identified by her name as the object of Lysidamus' desires. Her name is derived from *casia*, meaning "cinnamon." See MacCary and Willcock (1976), 126 *ad* 219.

anyone. Nothing can be pleasant or piquant, unless love is mixed in.

Love is an additive, which can change how something registers on the senses (the bitter made sweet, 223) without changing the nature of the thing. Lysidamus' perfume works much the same way: the old goat thinks he can become a sweet young thing merely by perfuming himself:

> myropolas omnis sollicito, ubiquomque est lepidum
>   unguentum, unguor,
> ut illi placeam; et placeo, ut videor. . . .   (226-27)

I pester all the perfume-sellers, and wherever there's a nice cologne to be had, I use it, just to please her—and I *do* please her, I think. . . .

The stock scene that now ensues between Lysidamus and Cleostrata might seem to undercut the idea of variation in the stock types of *matrona* and *senex*. Cleostrata *is* suspicious, Lysidamus defensive. Plautus is merely playing with us, just as Lysidamus and Cleostrata are playing with each other. This scene allows Lysidamus to bid for the audience's favor, to compete for the position Cleostrata presently holds. The asides make this clear: Lysidamus dominates them, and with them the laughs:

> CL. enicas.
> LY. *vera dicas velim.*
> CL.   credo ego istuc tibi.
> LY. respice, o mi lepos.
> CL.   nempe ita ut tu mihi es.
> unde hic, amabo, unguenta olent?
> LY.   *oh perii!*
>   *manufesto miser*
>   *teneor. cesso caput pallio detergere.*
>   *ut le bonu' Mercurius perdat, myropola, quia haec*
>   *mihi dedisti.*   (233-38)

CL. You're killing me.
(I wish I were.)
CL. There I believe you.
LY. Look at me, bunnykins.
CL. Just as you do me. Where did you acquire this smell of perfume, my dear?
LY. (Yipes! I'm caught red-handed. I've got to wipe my face on my sleeve. May Mercury murder that myrrh-seller, who gave me the goods!)

Lysidamus and Cleostrata are playing a game of angry wife and loving, dutiful husband, but Lysidamus drops his mask occasionally to let us know how he really feels: angry as well, but also fearful (266 *subolet, sentio*).[19]

The issue then shifts from Lysidamus' behavior to the fate of Casina. Lysidamus wants her for himself (ostensibly, though, for his slave Olympio), the *matrona* wants her for the son. This argument is in effect played out three times, twice on stage: first between Lysidamus and Cleostrata (252-74), then between Lysidamus and Chalinus (279-308), while simultaneously offstage Olympio and Cleostrata debate (reported 309-24). Each argument leaves the principals entrenched in their original positions. No movement is conceivable.

The allotment scene (353-423) caps and resolves this sequence of arguments. Lysidamus and Cleostrata agree to draw lots from a water-filled urn to determine to whom to award Casina. The appeal of this scene is obvious: it is both novel and spectacular.[20] The scene offers us a striking picture, with Cleostrata at the apex of a visual triangle of power: she holds the urn center stage, while Lysidamus and Chalinus hover nervously on either side of her. The scene visually foreshadows her subsequent central role in the play. There is also excellent opportunity for slapstick and physical comedy in the allotment scene as the two slaves, egged on by master and mis-

[19] Lambinus rightly attributes this to Lysidamus.
[20] MacCary and Willcock (1976), 35-38, believe that the structure of the *Casina* is built around three such "spectacular" scenes: the allotment, Pardalisca's messenger speech (612-718), and the wedding procession and aftermath (815-1018).

78

tress, come to blows (404ff.). Plautus introduces in this scene Lysidamus' unfortunate penchant for the Freudian slip, which will haunt him through the rest of the play:

LY. . . . Casina ut uxor mihi daretur; et nunc etiam censeo.
CL. tibi daretur illa?
LY.   mihi enim—ah, non id volui dicere:
 dum 'mihi' volui, 'huic' dixi, atque adeo mihi dum
     cupio—perperam
jam dudum hercle fabulor.   (365-68)

LY. . . . . that Casina should be married to me; and now I agree too.
CL. Married to *you?*
LY. Indeed to me—oops, that's not what I meant to say. When I wanted to say "to me," I said "to this fellow," even while I still want her for myself—damn it, I'm still talking nonsense!

Both rivalries, slave versus slave, master versus mistress, are present and fully displayed.

The only thing missing at first glance is an explanation of why the scene takes place at all. Why are the participants willing to submit what each believes to be his incontrovertible right to the fortunes of the lot? Lysidamus should have the clear legal right to decide the fate of any slave of his household by his *patria potestas*. Myrrhina, Cleostrata's friend, gives a neat summation of this doctrine in her advice to her friend (198-202), and Lysidamus himself claims this power vis-à-vis his son earlier in the play (263-65). Yet here he yields his power. Why? Because he is so afraid of his wife? If her power over him is so great, why does *she* agree to the lottery? She yields to his suggested solution without a single protest. This cannot be acceptance of his *patria potestas* at last. Is it then reverence for the gods and the justice of their decision through the lot? Given the event about to occur, this hardly seems likely.

The real reason is that the plot must be advanced—the necessity is dramaturgical. All the pedantic quibbles of the previous paragraph would not have occurred to an audience, even a Roman one familiar with *patria potestas*; but even had they noticed, the objection would not arise. Segal might say in the Saturnalian spirit of the day that *patria potestas* is overturned.[21] It will in fact take a literal beating at the end of the play.

It is also dramaturgical necessity and not the gods that gives Lysidamus and Olympio the victory, though the scene is filled with references to the gods and *pietas*.[22] The irreverence of the scene is heightened by the blasphemous byplay in which Lysidamus as "Jupiter" and Cleostrata as "Juno" set their slaves on each other. "Jupiter" gets the worst of it, which is indeed the shape of things to come.

Lysidamus has through the whole of the play until now been attempting to assume the mask and play the role of Jupiter. He has established a blustery control of the action, but this scene and two references which precede it have insinuated into the mind of the audience the notion that the throne of this king of gods and men is by no means secure. When Lysidamus first lays claims to the role of Jupiter, Olympio pointedly reminds him that he is only a mortal Jove. He is likely to leave his throne to lesser deities (331-36). A little further back there is a superficially less sinister but in the event more ominous reference to any would-be Jupiter. Olympio told Cleostrata, who was begging him to yield his claim to Casina, that he would not yield her even to Jupiter himself (323). Though the audience cannot yet know it, its mind is now alive to the possibility that Jupiter/Lysidamus, even if he gains Casina for Olympio, may not have thereby gained her for himself. We begin to see just to what degraded position Lysidamus' lust has driven him. It has been noted before that his role as *senex amator* parallels that of the *adulescens amans* in his dependence on the slave.[23] What has *not* been noted before is the qualitative difference in the situations of the usual penniless young lover and Lysidamus. Casina will be Olympio's wife, an estate neither Olympio nor we expect to be celibate. Lysi-

---

[21] Segal (1968), 24-25, calls this scene a husband/wife fistfight by proxy.

[22] Forms of *deus*: 389, 396, 417, plus numerous interjections of *hercle*. One wonders whether the frequent use of this oath is somehow a preparation for the brief reference to the myth of the descendants of Hercules made in 398. Forms of *pietas*: 383, 418.

[23] Forehand (1973), 242. On the scene at 725ff., see below.

damus, a respected *paterfamilias*, will be sharing a woman with a slave. Moreover, this particular design for living is not even comparable to the odd time-sharing arrangement Diabolus proposes at the end of the *Asinaria*. Whatever the realities, in the world of comedy the audience knows that no young girl will have any desire for Lysidamus if the younger and presumably more attractive Olympio is competing for her love. Already we know that Lysidamus is so degraded in his own estimation that he will accept such an inferior position.

The tension is wound tight, the lot falls, and Olympio is the victor. Lysidamus rejoices in one line

> L Y . quom nos di juvere, Olympio,
> gaudeo. (417-18)

> L Y . Since the gods are helping us, Olympio, I'm glad. . . .

and then falls at once to giving orders. The gods above seem to have ratified the will of Jupiter below.

Chalinus is left alone for a soliloquy (424-36). Once again, the very fact that it is a soliloquy is a direct challenge to the audience and an appeal for sympathy. He sorrows not at his own deprivation (one doubts that the young Euthynicus would have been so inclined to share Casina with *his* slave and agent, and Chalinus probably knew this) but at his opponents' joy. He is suspicious; the subsequent eavesdropping scene (437-514) confirms those suspicions and more.

Chalinus' asides in this scene have a very important function in guiding the audience's response to what it learns. If the scene consisted of Lysidamus and Olympio alone, we would merely have a very funny scene of horseplay and sexual humor. With Chalinus as commentator, the scene is integrated into the larger pattern of Lysidamus' enslavement to his lust.[24] The scene belongs to Chalinus as the figure with the power—of knowledge. As an audience be-

---

[24] In much the same way, Charmides from his superior position as eavesdropper comments on and interprets the appearance of Stasimus as the running slave in the *Trinummus*, 1008ff. Wright (1982), 519-20, has suggested that Stasimus is to be taken less than seriously in this scene; the staging, with Charmides as interpreter, reinforces this perception.

lieving our own knowledge of events in the play to be superior to that of the characters, we identify in the scene with Chalinus and *his* superior position of knowledge. Even in his moment of exultation, Lysidamus' power, seemingly confirmed by the lot, is in actuality beginning to slip.

The importance of the scene for Lysidamus' characterization is clear. He is a lecher of catholic tastes. In the midst of his desire for Casina, he makes a virtual assault on Olympio (452-59), and one of Chalinus' asides implies that he was also once the object of an attack-mixed-with-bribe made by Lysidamus:

> CH. illuc est, illuc, quod hic hunc fecit vilicum:
> et idem me pridem, quom ei advorsum veneram,
> facere atriensem voluerat sub janua.   (460-62)

> CH. There, there, *that's* why he made this fellow overseer!
> Once when I came here, he wanted to doormanize me on the doorstep.

Chalinus also uses a metaphor for Lysidamus and Olympio that is part of an important sequence in the play: they are wild boars whom he has now caught in a thicket:[25]

> CH. enim vero huc aures magi' sunt adhibendae mihi:
> iam ego uno in saltu lepide apros capiam duos. (475-76)

> CH. I'd better cock my ear to this; I'll neatly snare these two boars in one trap.

Chalinus' soliloquy (504-14), wherein he exults in his discovery, shows a fascinating transformation of character. He begins like the typical *servus callidus*: he would not trade his freedom, not even three freedoms, for this chance to concoct some mischief:

> CH. tribu' non conduci possum libertatibus
> quin ego illis hodie comparem magnum malum

[25] See MacCary and Willcock (1976), 153, and Forehand (1973), 245.

> quinque hanc omnem rem meae erae jam faciam
>   palam.
> manufesto teneo in noxia inimicos meos.
> sed si nunc facere volt era *officium* suom,
> nostra omnis lis est. pulchre praevortar viros.
> nostro omine it dies; jam victi vicimus.
> ibo intro, ut id quod alius condivit coquos,
> ego nunc vicissim ut alio pacto condiam. . . . (504-12)

I wouldn't trade three freedoms for the disaster I'll bestow
on them today, nor fail to expose this whole plot to my
mistress. I've got my enemies cold. Now if the mistress
wants to do her part, we've won the whole case. I'll turn
those guys inside out. We've turned the tables and won the
day. I'll go inside, where I'll rehash another cook's
concoction to my own taste. . . .

But how will he do it? He will tell the mistress (506); not only that,
it is then up to Cleostrata to perform her role (508 *officium*) properly, in order for the victory to be theirs. Without lines 506 and
508, Chalinus is as exultant and confident of wreaking his own
victory as Pseudolus, indeed using the same image for his activity:

> PS. illic homo meus est, nisi omnes di atque homines me
>   deserunt.
> exossabo ego illum simulter itidem ut murenam
> coquos.
>
> *Pseudolus* 381-82

> PS. The man is mine, unless all the gods and men desert
>   me. I'll debone him, just as a cook does an eel.

With lines 506 and 508, he is not the same sort of character at all.
   We have noted above the accumulating evidence that Lysidamus
is not a light-hearted old man whose fancy has turned to love, a
sympathetic Plautine reveller with whom our loyalties should lie.
In a very brief interchange with Alcesimus (515-30), Lysidamus

explicitly confirms this for us. He will have from his friend none of the reprimands and advice appropriate to apply to a *senex amator*:

> "cano capite" "aetate aliena" eo addito ad compendium,
> "quoi sit uxor," id quoque illuc ponito ad compendium.
>
> (518-19)

> "With your grey hairs"—"at your age"—just save your breath. "Your poor wife"—spare me that, too.

In rejecting these admonitions, he rejects the sympathetic role that goes with them. Lysidamus' sin is not sex; it is obsession.

We are now halfway through the play. The pace until now has been fairly slow. Only one thing has really happened: the award of Casina to Olympio by the lot. Lysidamus' plans are in motion, but Chalinus has found him out. The short scene between Lysidamus and Alcesimus is a moment of poised calm before the storm breaks.

The storm arrives in the person of Cleostrata (531). Her surprise and rage motivate her to do what no other *matrona* in Roman comedy does: to seize control of the plot and become for the remainder of the play the *poeta* in charge of the action. She starts simply, with a little masterly inactivity. Alcesimus has been told by Lysidamus that she will invite his wife Myrrhina over to help with the upcoming wedding; he says as much in 543. Cleostrata simply does not respond, politely putting him off and baffling him. She does it so skillfully that, though he momentarily wonders if she could suspect him and his function in Lysidamus' scheme, he dismisses the thought on the grounds that it would be out of character for her not to say anything about it to him (554-55)—as it certainly would be for the typical nagging wife. Cleostrata is the typical wife no longer.

Instead she is now the exultant gamester and plotter. Her soliloquy (558-62) is filled with terms from *ludo* roots: 558 *lepide ludifactus*, 560 *ludificem . . . delusi*. She looks forward to her next success, the delusion of her unsuspecting husband (560). Her control is further emphasized by her sheer presence: the soliloquies of both Alcesimus and Lysidamus are played under her baleful eye.

Her scene with her husband (576-90) shows her growing con-

fidence and control. She quickly ad-libs an explanation for Myrrhina's absence from the wedding preparations (which throws Lysidamus' plans into disarray), sowing discord by blaming this on
Alcesimus (580-83). Cleostrata has the audience on her side now,
as her parting aside, promising more fun to come, shows:

> jam pol ego huic aliquem in pectus iniciam metum;
> miserrumum hodie ego hunc habebo amasium.   (589-90)

> Now by heaven I've put a good scare in his heart; today I'll
> make this lover suffer.

The *Casina* is finally beginning to roll. The two elderly conspirators
both feel they have been made fools of (592 *me . . . ludifactust*)[26]
and fall to quarrelling. In the high-speed interchange of confused
and angry fragments of lines (from 603 to 611)[27] the fact that
Cleostrata has certainly lied to one of them comes out, but both are
too angry to notice.

Pardalisca's running entrance with the news that Casina has
gone homicidally mad (621-719) gives Lysidamus no time for later
reflection. In meter and manner her entrance parodies that of a
woman in distress in tragedy.[28] Indeed Pardalisca can virtually play
the mad scene herself in place of the absent/nonexistent Casina.
Plautus gives her full rein at first. She nearly overdoes her vapors,
as Lysidamus suspects for a moment he is being made a fool of (645
ludibrio . . . habuisti). She soon settles down to her narrative, which
is designed to scare Lysidamus silly. The asides which Plautus then
allows Lysidamus show that Pardalisca is succeeding in her attempt
(661, 665, 672, 682-83).

Finally the audience is let in on the secret; with the proper
playing-style on Pardalisca's part it may not have been much of a
secret, anyway. The entire tale is another game (685 *ludo*, 668

---

[26] They have, of course, not only been made fools of, but also have been
made into a play, a *ludus*, by the playwright Cleostrata.

[27] I prefer the division of 605-9 among the two speakers, as in the Nixon/
Leo Loeb text (1917), 66, to MacCary and Willcock's strict reliance on the
manuscripts. See, however, their note: MacCary and Willcock (1976), 165.

[28] MacCary and Willcock (1976), 170, *ad* 621-29.

ludere), a plot authored by Cleostrata with help from her neighbor Myrrhina.[29]

> PA. ludo ego hunc facete;
> nam quae facta dixi omnia huic falsa dixi:
> era atque haec dolum ex proxumo hunc protulerent,
> ego hunc missa sum ludere.   (685-88)

> PA. I'm finely fooling this fool. The deeds I've told are indeed undone. My mistress and her neighbor schemed this plot, and I've been sent to play it on him.

Lysidamus puts on a brave front and counsels persuasion, but his fear is evident.[30]

Olympio now appears with the cook and provisions for a wedding feast in tow (720-58). The scene is a typical one for a *servus gloriosus*, as Olympio now presents himself to be (723 *cesso magnufice patriceque amicirier*). He affects contempt for his master.[31] He denies his slave status (735-36), reminds Lysidamus of his promise of freedom (737), and effects a reversal of roles whereby he becomes the master and Lysidamus the slave (738-40). In this he and Lysidamus re-enact the usual scene of role reversal between young master and man.[32] There is an ironic difference, however. Olympio has done nothing to deserve such exalted status: he has displayed none of the cleverness that is the basis for such comic superiority. The

---

[29] Why Plautus gives "coauthor" status to Myrrhina is a bit of a mystery. It may simply be part of the pattern of doubling and symmetry in the play. The major characters function as allied or opposing pairs. The allies are the two *senes*, the two *matronae*, and the master and slave pairs. The oppositions are obviously the two slaves and the husband and wife.

[30] There is a nice irony in Lysidamus' *blande orato* of 707. This quality of persuasiveness is just what he accused his wife of lacking toward Alcesimus in 584. Both he and she were failures at persuasion when they originally tried to resolve the dispute over Casina by appealing to each other's slaves (274 *blandior*). Delusion, though, is a form of persuasion, and at that Cleostrata is now proving herself thoroughly adept.

[31] *Foetet tuos mihi sermo.* The use of *foetet* echoes the animal imagery we see applied repeatedly to Lysidamus.

[32] See Segal (1968), 113-14, on this scene in particular and his chapter 4, "From Slavery to Freedom," *passim*.

plan is Lysidamus'. Olympio is no more than a tool. His power is as patently hollow by now as Lysidamus', and the audience is thereby prepared for his coming overthrow. Lysidamus, by his dependence on such a sham as Olympio, is even more degraded in this scene.

Pardalisca returns (759-79) to report on the progress of the plot. Forehand rightly emphasizes the theatrical allusions (760 *ludos*, 761 *ludi ludificabiles*) in this speech.[33]

> PA. Nec pol ego Nemeae credo neque ego Olumpiae
> neque usquam ludos tam festivos fieri
> quam hic intus fiunt ludi ludificabiles
> seni nostro et nostro Olympioni vilico.   (759-62)

> PA. I'm sure that never at Nemea or Olympia have such festive games been played as the ludicrous antics of our old master and Olympio the overseer here inside.

By her soliloquy directly spoken to the audience, Pardalisca becomes a part of the audience looking in at the inner plot of the delusion of Lysidamus and Olympio. Moreover, we learn the key element of the farce to come: Chalinus, dressed up in veils, will be substituted for Casina (769-79). By sharing the audience's point of view, she encourages the audience in turn to share *her* sense of participation in making the play happen. Pardalisca remains for a few moments to banter with Lysidamus, then withdraws. Though he was earlier badgering the cooks about dinner (765-66), Lysidamus now, like the good young lover, proclaims he can live on love—even if he *is* starving (795). Olympio, who arrives next, is less inclined to put up with starvation, and says so twice (801-3). The imagery harks back to Lysidamus' first soliloquy on love as a spice (217ff.); he is now discovering that man does not live by spice alone; he needs food to which to add it. Comedy's vision of happiness includes both food and sex. The fact that both men do without their dinners foreshadows the frustration of their amorous desires. The animal imagery for Lysidamus recurs as Olympio compares him to an

---

[33] Forehand (1973), 246. The passage is also notable as the starting-point for Fraenkel's brilliant study of Plautine originality; see Fraenkel (1960), 7ff.

untamed horse; Lysidamus, ever insatiable, counters with a joke having homosexual overtones (811-13).

"Casina" is handed over to her two co-husbands in a scene clearly controlled by Cleostrata and her helper Pardalisca (815-54). Pardalisca opens with her superb parody of advice for a young bride (815-21). The reactions of the two men pointedly contrast: Olympio objects (since he will have to live with whatever behavior Casina adopts), while Lysidamus advises ignoring it. After all, he merely wants tonight's entertainment. Cleostrata bestows the bride on Olympio (829-30),[34] and the women withdraw. The two bridegrooms' first advances are met with force, but undeterred they carry "Casina" off to Alcesimus' house.

The women return, and their lines cap and make explicit the theatrical references we have seen before. Having dined well, they have now come out to see a play (856 *ludos visere*)! What play? Why, the one Cleostrata, with help from the other women, has improvised for the occasion, and a good one it is, too, in Myrrhina's opinion:

> nec fallaciam astutiorem ullus fecit
> poeta atque ut haec est fabre facta ab nobis.   (860-61)

No other poet has ever produced a sharper gimmick than this one we fabricated.

One wonders whether she is praising Cleostrata or Plautus—or if it really matters. It is the ladies' matinee today, and they sit back with their popcorn to watch the show, though Pardalisca has more work to do on the play (868 *ut ludibrio habeas*).

No summary can do justice to the comedy of the two ensuing monologues of Olympio (875ff.) and Lysidamus (937ff.). A few points only should be noted. Both men make rather direct appeals to the audience for help and sympathy. Olympio begs for the audience's attention in the second person much as a prologue asks for attention and indulgence for *his* play—one more way in which Cleostrata's fiction is structured as a play-within-the-play:

[34] See MacCary and Willcock (1976), 191, *ad* 829.

operam date, dum mea facta itero: est operae pretium
  auribus accipere,
ita ridicula auditu, iteratu ea sunt quae ego intus turbavi.

(879-80)

Pay attention while I tell my tale. It's worth the price of
admission, just to hear me tell the ridiculous uproars I
caused inside.

The second person is unparalleled in this play outside the prologue
and epilogue. Lysidamus in his misery seems to scan the crowd
looking for a substitute to take his place:[35]

sed ecquis est qui homo munus velit fungier pro me?

(951-52)

Is there any man willing to do my duty for me?

Both are further humiliated when they discover the onstage audience
and are interrogated by the women (Cleostrata naturally taking the
lead). Lysidamus' degradation to the status of a slave is complete,
since he now decides to become a fugitive slave in order to escape
a beating from his wife:

---

[35] See Nixon's translation in the Loeb (1917), 101-3, which goes a bit beyond
the text in a good cause. The idea is a comic staple; one thinks of Ko-Ko's
search for a Lord High Substitute to be executed in his place in Gilbert and
Sullivan's *Mikado*. This appeal to the audience in fact anticipates Lysidamus'
degradation to slave status (see below), for he here echoes Tranio in the *Mostellaria* 354-55:

ecquis homo est, qui facere argenti cupiat aliquantum lucri,
qui hodie sese excruciare meam vicem possit pati?

Is there anybody, who wants to make a buck today, who could take my place
at a crucifixion?

Other characters appeal for audience help in different ways. Euclio in the
Aulularia 715ff., appeals to the audience for help in locating his gold. Halisca
in the *Cistellaria* 678-81 asks for audience help in tracing the casket of the title
that contains the recognition tokens.

quid nunc agam nescio, nisi ut
inprobos famulos imiter ac domo fugiam.
nam salus nulla est scapulis, si domum redeo.   (953-56)

hac dabo protinam et fugiam.   (959)

I don't know what to do unless I imitate the rascal slaves and
run away from home. If I go home, my shoulders shall
suffer. . . . I'll take to the road at once and run.

It is in the status of slave who can be beaten for any future infractions
(1003) that he is finally accepted back by his wife.[36] Cleostrata has
one more reason for forgiving him, and a wonderfully metatheatrical
reason it is too: she has grown tired of the play of her own creation
and now wants to put the only possible ending to it:

hanc ex longa longiorem ne faciamus fabulam.   (1006)

So we won't make this play any longer than it is.[37]

Aside from the two or three lines of later summary of the
Greek play's plot (1012-14), the epilogue seems thoroughly Plautine. The appeal for applause is couched in a carrot-and-stick approach: applause will earn the applauder the right to happiness with
his mistress, while silence will earn him in place of his mistress a
smelly old goat.[38]

The play is over; our linear experience of Plautus' dramatic
poem is done. Once again, the structure has revealed itself as one
of shifting control of the plot. When the play opens, Lysidamus has
a plan (as does his absent son) to gain Casina for himself. He is
thus in a small way, though nowhere explicitly, a *poeta*. That plan
is, by luck (i.e., the lot) rather than its merits, carried near to

---

[36] Lysidamus is not restored to his place as *paterfamilias*. Cleostrata, by her
control of the plot, has usurped his place.

[37] A familiar Plautine joke: cf. *Mercator* 1007 and *Poenulus* 1224, where
Agorastocles jokes that the audience are getting thirsty.

[38] One last item in the sequence of animal imagery.

success. Cleostrata, whose independence and strong character are shown early on, also by luck learns of her husband's plan and sets a counterplot in motion; she is explicitly the *poeta* (861) of the second half of the play. By the superior merits of the plot of her play, she gains the victory. The average spectator, doubtless having had a good laugh at the characters' expense, thanks to Plautus, probably carries away with him only the details of a few of the more hilarious moments (Olympio's description of what he found in his bridal bed, say) and the conviction natural to Plautine drama that the smart ones finish first, and getting caught is the only crime. This spectator also doubtless believes with Sam Goldwyn "if you wanna send a message, call Western Union."

A few other spectators and we ourselves, though, are not content with this only. I believe there is a message around which the images, the role transferrals, and the reversals cohere. It is a message that comes into focus only at the very end of the play with a reference (repeated six times in four lines) to the Bacchantes:

L Y . Bacchae hercle, uxor—
C L .   Bacchae?
L Y .   Bacchae hercle, uxor—
M Y .   nugatur sciens,
                          nam ecastor nunc Bacchae nullae ludunt.
L Y . oblitus fui,
                  sed tamen Bacchae—
C L .   quid, Bacchae? . . .   (979-81)

L Y . I swear, my dear, the Bacchae—
C L . The Bacchae?
L Y . I swear, my dear, the Bacchae—
M Y . He knows he's babbling, for there are no Bacchae at play just now.
L Y . I forgot, but nevertheless the Bacchae—
C L . *What* Bacchae?

The lines have always been used to date the *Casina* after the famous *S. C. de Bacchinalibus* of 186 B.C. To my knowledge only

MacCary has gone further than the mere historical fact and attempted to read in these lines a poetic meaning within the social and historical context, a meaning he summarizes thus:

> Plautus uses sexual assault as a metaphor and example of the social, familial, and economic repression which Lysidamus as *paterfamilias* practices on his family; his reference to the Bacchae at the very end of the play must be understood in the context of this thematic development: Lysidamus has been caught sexually abusing a male slave and this he blames on the Bacchae, just as Livy blames all manner of sexual and moral corruption on those convenient scapegoats.[39]

MacCary thus sees Lysidamus as a repressive figure. Such figures are the enemy of comedy and their overthrow its goal. The connections and resonances of a reference to the Bacchae are much richer, however.

The core of the *Casina* is the old, old joke about the man who goes to bed with a woman, only to find out that "she" is a man.[40] Thus one can say that at heart the *Casina* is a play about sexual role reversal.[41] The *Casina* abounds in role reversals. The *senex* becomes the *adulescens amans*. In both these capacities he is *erus*, but he becomes by a further reversal *servus*, while his personal *servus* for a time becomes *erus* and *liber*. The slave Olympio thus becomes for a time a *servus gloriosus* but is finally humiliated and defeated as no true clever slave in Plautus is. Lysidamus nearly undergoes one final transformation, to fugitive slave,[42] before he is caught and brought back to his original role of *senex*.

Other role reversals are sexual reversals as well. The *matrona*

---

[39] MacCary (1975), 462-63. MacCary explains that it was widely believed that men were required sexually to abuse each other in the Bacchic initiation rites. Hence Lysidamus is about to explain his assault on Chalinus this way before he is interrupted.

[40] A recent exemplum is delightfully reported by Paul Theroux (1975), 211.

[41] After writing this chapter, I was very pleased to find many of my suggestions here confirmed and considerably elaborated by Chiarini (1978), who concentrates on the sexual imagery throughout the play.

[42] For it is the function of a slave to flee: cf. *Asinaria* 380: *quin tuom officium facis ergo ac fugis?*

becomes the *servus callidus* when she seizes control of the play. Her two allies, a *matrona* and an *ancilla*, take on roles usually played by fellow male slaves serving the *architectus doli*, the *servus callidus*. It may even be an artistically valid *post hoc, propter hoc* to argue that Cleostrata is led by her own sexual role reversal (a transition from passive to active in the world of Roman comedy) to the central idea of her *fabula*, the sexual role reversal of Chalinus into "Casina."

This structural pattern is knit to one pattern of imagery only at the moment of the Bacchae reference. Throughout the play others have compared Lysidamus and his lust to animals, usually untamed or untameable: 239 *cana culex*, 476 *apros*, 535 *vetulis vervecibus*, 550 *hirqui*, 811 *equos*.[43] Lysidamus' lust is not human, not a straying within the limits that society and comedy can tolerate, but animalistic, frenzied, Bacchic. Comedy, as Walter Kerr has said,[44] is about human limitations. Comic man struggles against his limitations, yet *needs* those limitations. It is tragedy that bursts through the boundaries and never looks back—or never can go back. Lysidamus' rejection of his usual role (shown by his rejection of the usual advice given to the *senex amator*, a character who has taken but one step outside his proper role) threatens to break out of the bounds of comedy.

Yet how can this be? Is not comedy about holiday and freedom from morality? Yes, but as holiday can only exist by the existence of contrasting working days, license implies also the bonds of morality. The *Casina* is a darker comedy than most of Plautus' other works, because it rides so near the edge of the genre. The darkness is further proof of its marginal character; Lysidamus' sin is not lechery, but lust so excessive and animalistic that it becomes sex without joy.[45]

---

[43] See also MacCary and Willcock (1976), 31.

[44] Kerr (1967), 146.

[45] The importance of Lysidamus within the play cannot be overemphasized. The best interpretation of his character, and even more importantly his effect on stage, is the brief introduction in Tatum (1983), 85-89. He suggests that Lysidamus in performance creates a sympathy we might not expect simply from reading the text. Even so we should not forget the threat Lysidamus represents to the system of comedy if his lust is not tempered and brought back within social control.

CHAPTER VI

The Double-Dealer ~ or ~ The Skin-Changer

Let me think: meet her at eight—hum—ha! I have it. If I can speak to my lord before, I will deceive them all and yet secure myself. 'Twas a lucky thought! Well, this double-dealing is a jewel.
—Maskwell in *The Double-Dealer*

EVER since E. W. Handley's publication of fragments of Menander's *Dis Exapaton*, the Greek source for Plautus' *Bacchides*, the *Bacchides* has been the subject of lively discussion.[1] Most treatments have centered on Plautus' omission of two short scenes between father and son in the Menandrean text.[2] Indeed many useful conclusions about Plautine methods can be made for the specific scenes preserved in Greek, but we are still far from a general theory of Plautine *vortere*.[3] Fascinating as these problems are, we shall not

[1] Handley (1968). For subsequent bibliography, consult Segal (1981). The best introduction to the play as play is Tatum (1983), 15-19.

[2] Handley (1968), 14-16; see also the much more detailed and quite valuable discussion of Clark (1976), 85-96.

[3] Handley's brilliant work has been called the most important Plautine philological discovery of the century. The initial surprise was that Plautus could be quite a literal translator at points. Subsequent discussions of the relations of the *Bacchides* and the *Dis Exapaton* have emphasized the significance of Plautine changes and additions. Clark (1976) argues that Plautus' omission of the two father/son scenes has the function of increasing the structural symmetry of the play. Wright (1974), 138-42, in examining the motif of the returning traveler in Plautus, shows that three of the four standard elements of such a scene have been added by Plautus to the Menandrean original. Pöschl (1973) suggests that Plautus has improved the character of Mnesilochus vis-à-vis that of Menander's Sostratos. Segal (1981), 395-97, has a convenient survey of the discussions of this important topic up to 1976.

The impact of Handley's discovery, however, should not be overstated. Certainly he did not do so, though others have. Segal (1981), 353, sounds an important cautionary note:

When this publication last reviewed the state of Plautine scholarship . . . ,

consider them directly. Our purpose here once again will be to consider the dramaturgical functioning of the Latin play as it stands.

This task is hampered at the outset by the loss of the introductory scenes, from which only fragments survive. The most recent reconstruction of the opening, that of Gaiser, postulates three lost scenes.[4] Pistoclerus has been commissioned by a letter from his friend Mnesilochus to locate Mnesilochus' *amica*, Bacchis, who has been taken by the *miles* Cleomachus to Athens. Mnesilochus plans to return to Athens and wishes his friend Pistoclerus to secure Bacchis' freedom from the captain and keep her secretly pending his return. In the first scene Pistoclerus meets the Athenian Bacchis, twin sister of Mnesilochus' *amica*, and her maid. In the second, he delivers a delayed prologue as monologue. In the third, the Samian Bacchis (Mnesilochus' *amica*) appears, accompanied by the slave of her captain. The narrative content of these scenes is doubtless correctly reconstructed in the main, but from the fragments we can say nothing about the dramaturgical functioning of the scenes.

As our surviving text opens (5), Pistoclerus and the two Bacchides hold the stage. They are not all in conversation, however. The two Bacchides are plotting together, while Pistoclerus waits nervously outside their scene, unable to hear their discussion. He voices his curiosity to the audience (38), then braves the women directly. He is wary of entrapment, though, as his imagery of bird-snaring (49, 51) and of Bacchis as a predator (55 *mala tu es bestia*) shows. So far he is firm—though the overblown rhetoric of 65-73 shows he doth protest too much.

The Bacchides need him as a source of revenue. They must raise the money to buy off the Samian Bacchis' captain through their

---

J. A. Hanson remarked that if Menander's *Dyskolos* had turned out to be the actual model for a Plautine comedy, his entire survey "would be utterly different." . . . And yet, despite Handley's exciting contribution, this new survey is not "utterly different" from Hanson's.

The most important impact of Handley's study, as Segal goes on to note, may well be its substantiation of what Fraenkel had already told us. We know very little for certain about the plot of the *Dis Exapaton*. What *were* the two deceptions, for example? Gaiser (1970), 78, favors the idea that these were the two letters, in which case the whole first deception could be Plautine invention. One is also inclined to ask: were there twin girls in Menander? The whole theme of twins and doublets may be Plautine elaboration as well.

[4] Gaiser (1970), 65-69. See also Bader (1970), 304-23.

own devices (or so they presently believe). When Bacchis' direct attempt at seduction fails, she tries a new device: let Pistoclerus *pretend* (75 *simulato*) to love her. Pistoclerus sees two possibilities:

utrum ego istuc jocon adsimulem an serio? (75)

Should I play it for a joke or seriously?

Whether he plays it as a joke or seriously, in both cases it would still be a role. His vanity and imagination are both aroused; by asking these questions he has already accepted the part. Bacchis' seduction has succeeded, and she can now begin to give him his stage directions (76-77). Pistoclerus' stage fright does not immediately disappear. He stands poised outside the role for one moment (85 *rapidus fluvius est hic*), as Bacchis does outside hers (86), but when Bacchis directly questions his courage (92), he submits and throws himself so thoroughly into his role as lover that he insists on paying for the party they will stage (97-99). Their plot well launched, the Bacchides can retire inside quite satisfied with themselves. Note that the hunting images metamorphose into fishing: Pistoclerus has been well hooked (102) and will not wriggle off.

The functioning of this scene within the play is very simple: seduction equals induction. The play cannot begin until all the performers move into the world of comedy and adopt their roles. Pistoclerus refuses the temptations of Bacchis as actual, physical temptations. When, however, he is offered the *role* of *adulescens amans*, he cannot resist. He is a perfect Roman in this: rigidly and vociferously moral in "real life," he surrenders himself joyously to the Saturnalian spirit *in the theatre*. Pistoclerus enacts what the Roman audience imaginatively experienced every time it saw a play of Plautus: the shedding of the heavy burdens of *pietas* and *gravitas* in favor of festival. The *Bacchides* is not a comedy until Pistoclerus makes it so. The lost beginning scenes and the first part of this scene stand outside the world of comedy, but the seduction/induction of Bacchis carries Pistoclerus and the audience into that world.

When Pistoclerus returns with his tutor Lydus and considerable provisions in tow (109ff.), comedy has free rein. He is obviously throwing himself into the role of *adulescens amans*. Equally does

Lydus play the outraged guardian of morals. There is in this scene a theme of the importance of names and their propriety to associated roles. Lydus is outraged at the first-name familiarity which Pistoclerus adopts toward him (138), but Pistoclerus insists that it is appropriate to Lydus' new role as confidant (139-42). In Pistoclerus' view, one cannot remain always in the same role in life:

non omnis aetas, Lydo, ludo convenit. (129)

Not every age is one for *ludus*, Lydus.

Not only is there a pleasant pun on Lydus' name; I suspect more than one meaning to *ludo*. On the surface Pistoclerus means he cannot forever remain a schoolboy, but the meaning of "game" or "play" is just under the surface. When he has left the schoolroom, Pistoclerus will have graduated to amorous sports—of the sort that plays are written about. Pistoclerus insists on his right to allot the roles in his present play: he is master (162). This consciousness of social role emphasizes the adoption of comic roles that makes the play possible. Pistoclerus' insistence on his role as master is immediately given an ironic twist by the entrance of Chrysalus (170ff.). Neither his mask nor his speech (170 *erilis patria*) allows for any ambiguity as to *his* role: the *servus callidus* has come to save the day. His returning traveller speech (i.e., the thanks to the gods customary after a safe voyage)[5] is radically compressed into seven lines and focussed on the needs of the moment: he does not wish to meet the *senex* until he has carried out his young master's commission.

Pistoclerus reappears (178), and he and Chrysalus quickly get down to business. Chrysalus is in charge from the first—he even cuts off Pistoclerus' welcoming speech and summarizes what Pistoclerus *would* say (184).[6] More exposition ensues: the discovery of the Samian Bacchis, the return of Chrysalus' young master Mnesilochus. When Pistoclerus is carried away by his tale, however, and expatiates on the devotion of Bacchis to Mnesilochus in four

[5] Actually, first the land, then Apollo, whose altar is nearby. Apollo, god of theatre and poetry, seems unusually appropriate to this play.

[6] I would suggest punctuating with a dash after line 183. The content of 184 suggests that it is an interruption.

clauses beginning with *immo* (207, 208, 209, 211), Chrysalus becomes impatient and criticizes Pistoclerus for overacting:

non res, sed actor mihi cor odio sauciat.   (213)

It's not the play but the player that gives me heartburn.

Chrysalus wants control not only over the plot but over the performance style as well. He closes the scene by dismissing Pistoclerus with two brisk imperatives (224 *abi . . . dicito*).

Chrysalus only has time to announce briefly (229-34) his intentions of defrauding old Nicobulus, Mnesilochus' father, before the *senex* himself appears (235ff.). Chrysalus' aside to the audience before approaching Nicobulus (239-42) not only bids for audience sympathy but also launches a key image in the play, gold:

extexam ego illum pulchre jam, si di volunt.
hau dormitandumst: opus est chryso Chrysalo.
adibo hunc, quem quidem ego hodie faciam hic arietem
Phrixi, itaque tondebo auro usque ad vivam cutem.
servos salutat Nicobulum Chrysalus.   (239-42)

(God willing, I'll neatly unravel him now. This is no time
to nap. The golden boy needs gold in hand. I'll approach
this fellow and make him into the ram of Phrixus today.
What's more, I'll shave him to the quick of his gold.) His
servant Chrysalus gives greetings to Nicobulus!

Chrysalus, the golden boy as the Greek root of his name proclaims him to be, needs gold for his young master. Nicobulus is the ram of Phrixus, due to be shorn of his golden fleece. Here as elsewhere the wordplay on Chrysalus' name brings us back to the idea of his role: the *servus callidus* always supplies the gold.

Mnesilochus had been sent by his father to collect a debt in Ephesus. Chrysalus now spins a superb tale for the old man, with repeated reversals of fortune, of their attempts to collect and escape with the money, only to be frustrated by pirates and forced to leave most of the money on deposit in Ephesus. The genius of the scheme

lies in Chrysalus' claim not to know how much money young Mnesilochus was able to retrieve. Since in fact they did collect the full
amount, Mnesilochus can now keep back as much as he wishes.
Clark notes the vivid use of ship imagery in this scene, first as the
pirate ship itself, then as a metaphor for the old man freighted with
deception.[7]

Chrysalus' monologue (349-67), following the old man's departure, is a beautifully structured transition. It begins as self-
congratulation, rising to a climax at 357: *quas ego hic turbas dabo!*
Then the tone changes as Chrysalus considers for a moment how it
might all go wrong. And how might it go wrong? If the old man
finds out,

> quid mihi fiet postea?
> credo hercle adveniens nomen mutabit mihi
> facietque extemplo Crucisalum me ex Chrysalo.   (360-62)

> What will happen to me then? By heaven, I think he'll come
> back and change my name at once from Chrysalus to
> Crossalus.   (translation after Nixon)

If Chrysalus must change his name, he will change his role in the
play. At the risk of vivisecting a perfectly good pun, we must note
that name implies *persona*, which in turn implies role. To lose the
first is to lose the second and third as well.

The fun is by no means over. We know that this scheme of
Chrysalus' will not work, even if we do not yet know how it will
come apart. For one thing, the play is not yet half over—which the
audience surely would know. For another, Plautus mutes the victory
strains of Chrysalus: his meters in the monologue are iambics and
trochaics, simple recitative meters, and not an exultant *canticum*—
the rhythm is wrong for a finale. And lastly, it has just been too
easy; complications must ensue.

One key point that comes out of the end of Chrysalus' monologue is easily, and I believe often, overlooked: Chrysalus improvises his entire tale and the scheme of fraud on the spot. He leaves
the stage in order to acquaint Mnesilochus with his brainstorm (366).

[7] Clark (1976), 89-91.

We are not, of course, intended to ask why Chrysalus and Mnesilochus did not devise a plan together on the long coasting voyage from Ephesus instead of leaving it to the last possible moment. The familiar Plautine sense of improvisation adds excitement and interest to the scene just past. Moreover, the need to acquaint others with the improvised tale afterwards opens numerous possibilities for complications.

Lydus now bursts from the house of the Bacchides. Segal cites Lydus first among the roster of Plautine agelasts.[8] Certainly he is unsympathetic: a figure of repression in a world of comic freedom. Note, however, that Plautus reinforces this impression structurally. Lydus is given a monologue that is *not* a soliloquy (368-84). His speech is entirely framed as an address to the offstage Pistoclerus (367 *Pistoclere*). Were this a true soliloquy he could step to the footlights and make his plea for Roman virtue to the groundlings out front—and might very well appeal to some. Plautus insists rather that he shout at and plead with the silent, disdainful door.[9] He looks ridiculous and therefore sounds so: the staging undermines his standing with the audience. His exiting threat, though, promises more fun to come.

Mnesilochus himself now appears, moralizing and congratulating himself and his slave as he goes (385ff.). We gain the essential information that Chrysalus has informed him both of the tale about the gold and the discovery of Bacchis.

Lydus returns, dragging Philoxenus the father of Pistoclerus behind (405ff.). Mnesilochus for the moment steps into the background to eavesdrop, thereby reinforcing his kinship with the audience and allowing his comments to color the scene for us. The isolation of Lydus the agelast in this comic world is soon underscored.

---

[8] Segal (1968), 71-74.

[9] This setting of course has a long history in Greek poetry, usually for the young lover outside his mistress' door. Parody is possible here. In any case the theatrical functioning of the scene is very different from that in lyric. The *Curculio* (1ff.) opens with Phaedromus outside his mistress' door, but Plautus provides him with a slave Palinurus, whose function is to mock his master's lament to the door. Antipho in the *Stichus* 58ff. is introduced to us through an address to those within which is structurally similar to Lydus' speech. In the *Stichus* it reinforces our aversion to the harsh and unsympathetic character of Antipho.

Even Philoxenus will not back Lydus to the hilt—for he confesses to having been an *adulescens amans* once himself (410). Mnesilochus learns enough through his eavesdropping to grow anxious for his friend's reputation, as his asides show (414-15, 435-36, 449-50), while Lydus rants on. Mnesilochus unfortunately does not know as much as we the audience do. He assumes Pistoclerus is unjustly accused on account of the Samian Bacchis, an obligation undertaken for himself. When the reversal comes (477-88), the impact is severe: 489 *perdidisti me, sodalis.* . . . He delivers this aside but is overheard. Knowing his generous nature, though, Lydus and Philoxenus assume his distress to be purely selfless and depart.

Mnesilochus' soliloquy which follows is a study in comic incoherence (500-25). At first, despite his anger, he cannot quite forego his role as lover. There are three successive couplets with essentially the same *paraprosdokeion* joke: "I'll be revenged on her—by loving her" (505-6, 507-7a, 508-9). Such a hopelessly trapped lover is Argyrippus in the *Asinaria*. But then—

> sed satine ego animum mente sincera gero,
> qui ad hunc modum haec hic quae futura fabulor?   (509-10)

> Can I be in my right mind, dramatizing the future in this way?

He refuses to spin such play plots for himself (*fabulor*) and the role of helpless lover they entail, and adopts a desperate measure. Since he cannot rely on his own powers to resist Bacchis' blandishments, he will simply give all the money back to his father (520)—and in a stroke the whole plot so far is undone. Mnesilochus has not the power to create his own plot, to be his own poet, but he has the negative power to undo the plot of Chrysalus. In a destructive way he does manage to take control for a moment of his own destiny. Generous to the last, he also remembers to protect his accomplice Chrysalus from the father's wrath (521-23).[10]

[10] A great deal of attention has naturally been paid to this soliloquy and its relations to two soliloquies for Sostratos (= Mnesilochus) in Menander's *Dis Exapaton*. See especially Handley (1968), Gaiser (1970), Questa (1970), 191ff. For our purposes it suffices only to note that Plautus has created both the

The dramatic lapse of time is sufficiently indicated by a short entrance monologue for Pistoclerus (526-29); then Mnesilochus returns, his purpose carried out (530ff.). A confused and angry recognition duet makes clear the collapse of the first plot of the play, as Mnesilochus learns of the existence of two Bacchides.

Into this dramatic void steps the parasite of the *miles* like a new prologue (573ff.)—the play must begin again.[11] The parasite's demand for "your money or your girl" restates the fundamental problem: the Samian Bacchis needs money to buy off the captain, and as soon as possible. Though Pistoclerus succeeds in driving away the parasite in a scene of boisterous slapstick and verbal invention (583-605), that solves nothing either, as Pistoclerus' brief soliloquy tacitly acknowledges (606-11). Mnesilochus bursts from the house and soliloquizes on his folly (613-39). (Mnesilochus has a taste for soliloquy.) He arrives expatiating on friendship (385-404), later bursts into unreasoned anger at his father's supposed perfidy (500-25), and then repents at leisure. Clark has pointed out the predominance of the theme of friendship and enmity in his speeches.[12] These speeches characterize him as an unworldly young man who tends to think in abstracts. Small wonder, then, that he is in despair and at a loss for a course of action. He refuses to be consoled, and rejects Pistoclerus' faith that some god will aid them (638 *deus respiciet nos aliquis*) with the bitterly scornful word: *nugae!*

Into this critical moment steps their *deus ex machina*, Chrysalus. Chrysalus' first words lay claim to divine honors:[13]

---

paraprosdokeion jokes and more importantly the language of playmaking. Nothing in the Greek text parallels or even suggests the *fabulor* in 510. Nor does Syros (= Chrysalus) need the son's protection from the father in the *Dis Exapaton*. The old man utters no threats and seems only concerned to recover his money.

[11] The only comparison for such a complete re-beginning of a play that I can find is Euripides' *Helen*, where Menelaus' entrance, after the highly unusual departure of the chorus along with the principals, seems like a second prologue. The *Miles Gloriosus*, 596ff. has a partial new beginning with the departure of Sceledrus and the initiation of a new trick. The *Amphitruo* by contrast is constantly beginning anew; virtually every appearance of the two gods functions like a prologue, initiating a new action or providing new information.

[12] Clark (1976), 95.

[13] See Segal (1968), 132-36, on the *topos* of the slave as god. On the con-

hunc hominem decet auro expendi, huic decet statuam statui
ex auro. (640)

This man's worth his weight in gold; a golden statue ought
to be erected to him.

This splendid self-celebration of the *servus callidus* is a gold mine
of significant words, images, and themes. The gold, of course, comes
first as fact and image (640). Chrysalus wants his golden nature to
be honored with gold, to be physically exemplified. Next, Chrysalus
claims to have performed a double deed and earned double spoils
(641). The deeds are double in that on one hand they harm the
senex, on the other they benefit the son—but the former is more
important.

erum majorem meum ut ego hodie lusi lepide, ut
ludificatust! (642)

How I've played my old master for a fool today, how he's
been ludicrized!

He proclaims his own cleverness (643 *callidis dolis*), which will
bring him the comic trinity of food, drink, and love (646).
Now follows a passage of metatheatricality unparalleled in Plautus:

non mihi isti placent Parmenones, Syri,
qui duas aut tris minas auferunt eris. (649-50)

Don't give me those Parmenos, those Syruses, who bilk their
masters of two or three bucks.

The surface metatheatricality has always been visible: Chrysalus
proclaims his contempt for those stock Greek clever slaves who can

---

temporary significance of gold statues and honors in Rome, see Hanson (1965),
56.

only manage petty theft. He poses for the moment as dramaturg, implying the superiority of his own poetic self-creation to the work of other authors.[14] It is a moment of supreme self-consciousness in art.

We now can see that the lines demonstrate an even more important sense of metatheatre. The name of the slave in Menander's *Dis Exapaton* was Syrus.[15] There is more here than an in-joke for those who know the Greek text: it is the very paradigm of metatheatre, a character arguing with his own Ur-text! Chrysalus believes it is the function of art to improve on art. What he once was in Menander strikes Chrysalus as insignificant and contemptible. For his new incarnation he needs a new name and a new *persona*.

His superiority to his Greek counterparts lies in his brains, his *multipotens pectus* (652). Herein is his power to transform himself, to recreate himself in his own mental likeness—and what a powerful image Plautus uses for this process: the *vorsipellis* (657), the skin-changer.[16] The powers of the clever slave are supernatural. Through his self-transformations he controls those around him; he is invested with magic. On this crescendo the celebratory part of the soliloquy ends, and the transition back into the play begins.

Chrysalus expresses to the world at large his interest in the success of Mnesilochus' part of the plot: how much money did he keep for himself (663-66)? At this point he notices the two young men who have dutifully stood aside all this while and let a poet soliloquize. In a playful touch he returns to the image of gold/money that opened his soliloquy by asking Mnesilochus if he has dropped some coins and therefore gazes so intently at the ground (668).

[14] Fraenkel (1962), 236, took it as proof of Plautine aggrandizement of the part, which it certainly is, but there is much more.

[15] Handley (1968), 9.

[16] One should insist on this translation, I think. Though a *versipellis* is merely a werewolf in Petronius 62, Apuleius (*Metamorphoses* 2.22.6) presumes the same meaning as here: the magical ability to transform into anything ("... *deterrimae versipelles in quodvis animal ore converso latenter arrepant* ..."). When Mercury in *Amphitruo* 123 calls Jupiter a *vorsipellem*, he clearly implies the same breadth of power as does Apuleius; certainly the audience would be familiar with a range of animals into which the king of the gods had transformed himself in the course of his many amours. I had thought of alluding here to Beorn, the skin-changer in J.R.R. Tolkien's *The Hobbit*, but I have been strenuously advised against it.

The awful truth that Mnesilochus in a fit of pique has returned all the gold to his father comes out in a few lines (671-80). The agitation and confusion this occasions is marked beautifully by 681, where the speaker changes four times within one line:

CH. reddidisti?
MN.   reddidi.
CH.   omnene?
MN.   oppido.
CH.   occisi sumus.

CH. You returned it?
MN. I returned it.
CH. All of it?
MN. Altogether.
CH. We're done for!

Chrysalus fears the old man's wrath one moment (686-88),[17] makes a joke of it the next (689), but he is not at all happy about having it start the whole play over again:

MN. . . . nunc hoc tibi curandumst, Chrysale.
CH. quid vis curem?
MN.   ut ad senem etiam alteram facias viam.
    compara, fabricare, finge quod lubet, conglutina,
    ut senem hodie doctum docte follas aurumque auferas.
CH. vix videtur fieri posse.
MN.   perge, ac facile ecfeceris.
                                              (691-95)

MN. Now you must take care of this, Chrysalus.
CH. You want me to . . .?
MN. To make another inroad on the old man. Compilate, fabricate, create what you will, conglutinate, just so you con that confident old man and get the gelt.

---

[17] The Chrysalus/Crossalus wordplay, as Nixon has so brilliantly rendered it in the Loeb, recurs at 687. Chrysalus' name is constantly in our ears during the play, and usually is being punned upon.

CH. It scarcely seems possible.
MN. Forge on, and you'll easily accomplish it.

There can scarcely be a better definition of poetic activity than the series of imperatives in 693. "Conglutinate" seems especially appropriate to the metatheatrical pastiche techniques of improvisatory poets like Chrysalus and Plautus. At first Chrysalus seems to despair (695). Yet when Mnesilochus reluctantly reveals how fanatically suspicious the old man now is of Chrysalus (699-700), Chrysalus rises to the challenge on the instant: he cannot resist the opportunity to use Nicobulus' own humor against him (701).

The change of control of the play from the *adulescens* who has botched it to the *servus callidus* who will save the day is sharply marked. Mnesilochus immediately submits himself to the orders of his *imperator* (702),[18] and Chrysalus takes charge. Chrysalus says:

quid refert Chrysalo esse nomen, nisi factis probo? (704)

What good's a name like Chrysalus, unless I prove it with deeds?

Once again we are reminded that for Chrysalus name implies role. He must live up to his name by golden deeds. The military imagery first hinted at in the gold victor's statue of the first monologue (640) now flowers into a complete vision of seige and assault on the *senex*, who becomes an ancient walled city (709-13).[19]

The scene that ensues is full of Plautine improvisation. Chrysalus orders Pistoclerus from the stage to obtain . . . and then hesitates as if to think what he might use (714). Pistoclerus breaks in with a prompting *quid?* Writing materials, decides Chrysalus (715). Mnesilochus wants details of the plan immediately (716), but Chrysalus puts him off, a delay that leads to Chrysalus' discovery of the twin Bacchides. When Pistoclerus returns, Chrysalus seems

[18] In the attribution of 702 to Mnesilochus I stand with Nixon/Leo over against both Lindsay and Questa (1965). I can only appeal for authority to the superior dramatic effect of the transfer of power with this attribution, but that will suffice.

[19] On military imagery in the play in general see Clark (1976), 91, and MacCary (1968), 162-74.

momentarily to have forgotten what he ordered (727 *quid parasti?*), then begins to dictate a letter.

Every joke and strategy of the dictation scene in later drama has a germ here. Chrysalus seems on the point of beginning twice (728, 731) but does not do so; on the third try he can only tell his secretary Mnesilochus to write whatever salutation he will (731). Chrysalus pauses to reprove Pistoclerus for an interjection (732), then must have what he did not dictate read back to him. Inspiration suddenly bursts forth so fast that Mnesilochus cannot keep up (735-37); it is interesting to note that Plautus pays attention to the strict realism of the dictation process only in order to make a joke of it. The curious contents of the letter, warning Nicobulus of plotting by Chrysalus and even asking the old man to bind the slave, puzzle Mnesilochus, but Chrysalus will not explain (749-52). He and we must be content to await the event.

This dictation scene is unique in Plautus and seems to be unprecedented.[20] Other slave heroes use letters that fall into their hands by chance or *forge* letters offstage. Chrysalus dictates a letter onstage—which is *not* a forgery. It purports to be from Mnesilochus

[20] The only parallel for writing during a scene in the ancient theatre that I can find occurs in that most metatheatrical of Aristophanes' plays, the *Thesmophoriazusae* (on its metatheatricality, see Zeitlin [1982], 169-217). In 768-84, the old kinsman of Euripides attempts to imitate Palamedes in the Euripidean play of that name by carving appeals for help on wooden dedicatory plaques (instead of Palamedes' oars). The old kinsman (whose name, one notes with interest, is Mnesilochus) is attempting to recreate an extant play (the *Palamedes*) to get him out of his current difficulties, while Chrysalus is writing a new play.

The *Iphigenaia in Aulis* is more problematic. If we read the opening in the transmitted order (see Knox [1972], 239-61), the old man's use of the present tense form *grapheis* (35) in addressing Agamemnon might seem to imply that we have seen or are seeing Agamemnon writing and rewriting his second letter to Clytemnestra. Agamemnon himself speaks of revising the letter in the present: 108 *metagrapho* (in defense of which verb see Knox [1972], 258-59). We confront the old dilemma: if the character says he is performing an action, does he in fact enact it or leave it to the imagination? Taplin (1978), 16, clearly favors the former. Here I suspect that the writing was left to the imagination and the more easily depicted gesture of sealing and unsealing the letter (also referred to in 37-39 and 109-110) used to represent both actions.

These are minor quibbles, however: Agamemnon is imaginatively (if not realistically) conceived of as writing this second letter on stage. Agamemnon

to his father, and he does physically inscribe the letter. The hands are the hands of Mnesilochus, but the voice is the voice of Chrysalus.

In this scene Chrysalus changes from an improvisatory playwright (a player first among equals) to a literary one. Ancient poets usually dictated. Chrysalus is dictating a play here: directly, by writing a speech for Mnesilochus, and indirectly, as the subsequent course of the play is shaped by the letter. A wonderful irony therefore underlies this purported warning in the letter:

sed, pater, vide ne tibi hodie verba dat: quaeso cave.   (744)

But father, take care he doesn't make a fool of you; I beg you, beware.

The Latin idiom *verba dare* (to deceive, make a fool of) comes alive in this context. Chrysalus is literally "giving words" to the *senex*: fictive words, poetic words, deceptive words, which will most certainly make a fool of the old man. The giver of words is a playwright; the recipient is only a mouthpiece, a player.

Chrysalus' plan depends on the old man being angry to the point of irrationality, as he now reminds the audience (761-69). Nicobulus bursts forth in fine fury which Chrysalus welcomes thus:

salvos sum, iratus est senex.   (772)

I'm safe, the old man is angry.

This is a brilliant theatrical pun, with many resonances, on a recent famous saying that later became a well-known Roman proverb: *salva res est, saltat senex.*[21] The origin of the proverb lies in the story of an aged mime actor who in the Apolline games of 211 B.C. continued

---

is caught by the tragic implications of metatheatre. Having once written his own play by the first letter to Clytemnestra, he now hesitates too long over his rewriting of the play through this second letter. The metatheatrical implications of the letters in *Iphigenaia in Aulis* deserve further consideration elsewhere.

[21] See the discussion in Duckworth (1952), 13, of the proverb itself. He cites the sources in Festus (436ff., Lindsay's edition) and Servius (*ad Aen.* 8.110). I do not believe the pun here has been noticed before.

dancing to the flute despite a war scare that impelled all the spectators from the theatre, thereby preserving the ritual and eliminating the need for repetition. The functions of this pun are multivalent. On a simple level it sets the religious aura of the proverb against the petty and hilarious anger of Nicobulus. The theatrical context of the original proverb reminds us that the *senex* Nicobulus' anger is just as "theatrical" as the ritual dancing in the mime—and just as necessary. If the *senex* here is not angry, the play cannot go on, any more than the Apolline games could have continued had the *senex* there stopped the dance. Finally the animating humor of the whole reference is irony: Chrysalus is saved by the old man's wrath against him.[22]

A rich irony pervades the scene as well. Nicobulus believes that he is deceiving Chrysalus by withdrawing calmly (794) to fetch slaves to bind him. In fact it is Chrysalus who is master of the deception. He laughs to himself over the old man's belief that he (Nicobulus) could possibly be the playwright (795 *ut mihi verba dat*) instead of the manipulated player. Chrysalus' solemn assent to his servile status cannot but point the irony (791 *scio me esse servom*).

Now it remains for Chrysalus only to spring the trap, and this he does easily (799-841). By showing Nicobulus his son in the arms of Bacchis, Chrysalus diverts the old man's furious suspicion from himself to the son. Chrysalus fans the suspicion by refusing further information (840-41), a strategy that will not work for long, however.

Into this critical moment blusters the *miles* Cleomachus, enraged by the treatment accorded his parasite and out for vengeance (842ff.). With this timely (844 *per tempus*) arrival Chrysalus has materials for further improvisation: he tells Nicobulus that the soldier is the *vir* of Mnesilochus' mistress (851). Chrysalus plays with the declaration: *vir* might not mean "husband." When Nicobulus presses for precision (852 *nuptan est illa?*), Chrysalus dodges with irony (853 *scies haud multo post*). After all, the truth is the best kind

---

[22] Also, the fact that the *senex* is *iratus* is a theatrical given: it is in his mask. Unless Nicobulus changed his mask (we have no evidence that changing emotional states were ever depicted by changing the masks, a process likely only to confuse the audience), we the audience have known from his first entrance that he was a *senex iratus*. Chrysalus' humor is very dry.

of lie. Chrysalus' offer to negotiate for Nicobulus (861) is accepted quickly. Chrysalus strikes a deal, then carefully prompts both the others through their lines (881-83), allowing neither quite to realize what is transpiring.[23] He sends the soldier packing with rich abuse and tremendous oaths (884-904), then begs permission (!) to go in and reprimand Mnesilochus for his "misbehavior" in the strongest possible terms. His expression for doing this cites two famous characters of the comic stage, Clinias and Demetrius:[24]

> . . . plura ex me audiet hodie mala
> quam audivit umquam Clinia ex Demetrio. . . .   (911-12)

> . . . he will hear more harsh words from me than Clinias
> ever did from Demetrius.

Once more we are reminded that we are watching a play.

Nicobulus steps aside to reread the letter, still expressing doubts about Chrysalus (913-24), but Chrysalus himself returns to celebrate in his great victory *canticum* (925-78). The imagery of this speech is rich to the point of confusion. The play's preceding military imagery is linked to the general idea of assault on a walled city, and that city is Troy.[25] The soliloquy is also rich in parodistic possibilities. Take for example 935:

> O Troia, o patria, o Pergamum, o Priame periisti senex.

> O Troy, o native strand, o Pergamon, o Priam, fallen
> father.

The sounds of *p*'s, *t*'s and *r*'s mingle in rich confusion. The *o* is repeated at least once too often for tragic sincerity, and would allow a tragic pose on each repetition. Such a line gives an actor the opportunity to send up the whole tragic genre or alternatively parody

[23] In a somewhat similar fashion, the slave Stasimus in the *Trinummus* 402-590 guides his master through the betrothal negotiations for his sister, duping in the process both his master Lesbonicus and the other party, Philto.

[24] Or so we conclude them to be; see Ernout (1935), 110 *ad* 911.

[25] Cf. Segal (1968), 129-31, and Fraenkel (1960), 61ff., on this passage and such imagery in Plautus generally.

some rival actor's style. We know Chrysalus to be a severe critic of acting style from 213-15. Much of the humor is based on identifications of characters in the *Bacchides* with characters from the Trojan cycle, but these identifications shift rather rapidly. Nicobulus is now the city, now Priam, now a war captive for sale, now Priam again. Other characters and events change identities as rapidly. This is only to be expected, as a consistently maintained set of equivalences would be tedious and pedantic.[26]

This monologue seems to show Chrysalus at the peak of his power, but in the duplicitous spirit of the moment he intends to duplicate his first letter trick in order to obtain yet more money for Mnesilochus (969-72). Nicobulus has been lost in rereading that first letter and only now hears Chrysalus' voice (979), in itself a good joke.[27] In fact, Nicobulus' presence on the stage is the contin-

[26] I am afraid this is just what Jocelyn (1969), 135-52, would prefer. In keeping with my principle of confining the subterranean wars over *contaminatio* and *retractatio* to the footnotes, I shall answer some of his points here. Jocelyn has done a real service in minutely describing the shifts within the monologue, but all or nearly all are within the imaginative range of one poet and the performance powers of one actor. Jocelyn believes that separate image sequences denote separate conceptions and separate hands in the composition of Chrysalus' monologue. For example, he insists that the imagery of besieging a walled city is to be distinguished from Trojan imagery: "A theatre audience would have kept it quite separate from the comparison of events with the legendary capture of Troy" (141). There is simply no evidence for this assertion.

The contrast of future and perfect tenses in 929-31 disturbs Jocelyn also, but there is no dramatic inconsistency in taking 929 as a reference to the deception underway and 931 to the first deception. That may not be "logical" ordering by some standards, but with gesture and posture the actor can easily point the differences.

Similarly Jocelyn's objection to a "contradiction" between 929-30 and 937-40 will not hold. When Chrysalus claims to have gained the victory *sine classe sineque exercitu*, Plautus has not thereby forfeited the possibility of later identifying other figures from the Achaean army with characters. Neither he nor Aeschylus (cf. Aristophanes' *Frogs* 1152ff.) will be shackled to such literalism.

Some interpolation by actors (as Jocelyn suggests, 145, though I do not endorse his specific judgment there) is not impossible. However, to assume that *any* factual or stylistic inconsistency is proof of *retractatio* is to retreat to the nineteenth century. The "dramatic rationality" Jocelyn yearns for here (151) and would eagerly foist onto Plautus is a dull, dead thing indeed, fit for the study, not for the stage.

[27] During the soliloquy of Chrysalus, both he and Nicobulus stand outside the play, in separate imaginative spaces. Though such a conception of non-

uation of a challenge to Chrysalus' powers, a visual expression of the doubts expressed verbally at 922. The play is not yet over; Chrysalus has not completely won.

Chrysalus plays Nicobulus on his fishing line with exquisite care. By reverse psychology Chrysalus uses Nicobulus' suspicions to orchestrate the scene while the master seems to give the orders. Chrysalus attempts to leave; Nicobulus orders him to stay—exactly where Chrysalus wants to be to guide the response of the *senex* (988-90). Chrysalus advises against giving Mnesilochus the money and, somewhat prematurely, refuses to carry the money if Nicobulus does give it (1001-4). He protests so much that Nicobulus must demand quiet in which to read (1027). Nicobulus, his earlier doubts swept away by new events, decides to provide the money to prevent scandal and departs to get it. He returns and "forces" Chrysalus to take the money, then leaves (1066).

References to the Trojan War in asides have recurred through here (987, 1053ff.), but at his final exit Chrysalus is a thoroughly Roman conqueror, who even refuses a triumph (1067-75). Part of this passage deserves careful study:

> sed, spectatores, vos nunc ne miremini
> quod non triumpho: pervolgatum est, nil moror.   (1072-73)

> But spectators, don't be surprised that I'm not celebrating a triumph. It's too common—not for me.

This is the only formal piece of direct audience address Chrysalus has.[28] It comes at the climax of his control of the action. It comes when the audience expects something to top the great fall-of-Troy soliloquy—and it is a throwaway. Fraenkel is surely right in seeing this refusal to play triumphing general as an artistic, not historical, allusion.[29] I find it hard to be sure, however, that it is merely a

---

illusory playing may seem alien to late nineteenth- and early twentieth-century realistic modes of theatre, it has as a parallel Theopropides in the *Mostellaria* III. ii.

[28] I.e., with the use of *vos*. Lines 213-15 and 649-50 are self-conscious but not so framed.

[29] Fraenkel (1960), 226ff.

rejection of a convention grown stale, Plautus criticizing his imitators or even himself. Chrysalus' rejection of his expected role is
much more than that.

It may be Plautus' disclaimer, a refusal even to attempt to top
the great fall-of-Troy monologue. It is another *paraprosdokeion* joke,
then. The audience expects another lay-'em-in-the-aisles soliloquy,
and Chrysalus just figuratively waves and dives out the back entrance—never to reappear.[30] In all comedy I can think of only one
parallel to it: Alceste's final exit in the *Misanthrope* of Molière. The
scene in the *Bacchides* is indeed not so bleak by any means; Chrysalus
leaves them laughing as he goes. Alceste's flight from human society
is much more disturbing for its passion, but both Alceste and Chrysalus finally refuse to be bound to the conventional roles their plays
have assigned them. Millamant in *The Way of the World* may consent
to dwindle into a wife, but Alceste will not dwindle into a husband.
He will escape first. Chrysalus is tired of playing the *servus gloriosus*.
What he will escape to is not at all clear. Nonetheless, the protean
skin-changer will not content himself with the same repertoire.
Walter Kerr's judgment on the end of the *Misanthrope* may be
apposite: "Comedy is over, too, now, at the very end of the play.
One of the principals has refused to be contained by it."[31]

The leading character has made his escape. This gives a curious
tone and emphasis to the fact that the show must and does go on.
The double plot reasserts itself, as first Philoxenus (1076ff.), then
Nicobulus (1087ff.), returns. The speeches are deliberately contrasted, Philoxenus slightly worried about his son but expressing
confidence in Mnesilochus' ability to reclaim him (1084-86), Nicobulus gibbering with rage at Chrysalus (1094). Both show them-

---

[30] His absence from the play's finale is not unique but certainly is unusual.
Pseudolus, Toxilus, Cleostrata, and Epidicus are all on hand at the end of their
respective plays. Libanus and Leonida are not onstage at the end of the *Asinaria*,
but confusion of artistic control seems to be an organizing principal in that
play; it would be difficult to assert confidently that they are the only *architecti
doli* in it. The case of the title character in the *Curculio* is puzzling. The
manuscripts do not give him a part in the final scene of his play (679-729),
but neither is there any indication that he has left. See the edition of Wright
(1981), who suggests *ad* V.3 and *ad* 696 *et* 712 that certain lines should be
reassigned to Curculio in this final scene.

[31] Kerr (1967), 261.

selves the enemies of *ludus*, however. Philoxenus opposes too much fun and games for his son:

> . . . sed nimi' nolo desidiae ei dare ludum. (1083)

> But I don't want to give too much play to his desires.

Nicobulus' bitterest objection is to being made fun of:

> . . . hoc est demum quod percrucior,
> me hoc aetatis ludificari, immo edepol sic ludo factum. . . .
>
> (1099-1100)

> That's what really gripes me, at my age to be ridiculed, even more to be made a fool of. . . .

They recognize each other as twins in age and misfortune (1108). They then hail the Bacchides from the house.

What follows is another seduction/induction scene. One of the enduring problems of comedy is how to create the sense of an ending. The most enduring solution is to end by beginning again.[32] A marriage, that staple of comic finales from Peithetairus and Basileia in the *Birds* through Beatrice and Benedick, Ernest and Gwendolen, and 1930's screwball comedies, down to the more irregular arrangement for three that closes *Entertaining Mr. Sloane*, is a ritual and social re-beginning. Through a new family, life literally begins again.

As the Bacchides seduce the two old men, however, the feeling of the scene is quite different from a marriage re-beginning. For one thing, a relationship with a courtesan could never lead to marriage, unless in New Comedy fashion she is discovered to be a citizen after all. There is no hint of that in the *Bacchides*. Rather, it is

---

[32] The example that leaps to mind is Molnar's *The Guardsman*, with the dialogue of the opening scene repeated word for word as the curtain falls, but examples could be multiplied indefinitely. Perhaps this ability to join beginning to end is the source of comedy's immortality. Aristotle reports that Alcmaeon asserted that men die because they cannot join the beginning to the end (*Probl.* 17.3.916a33).

seduction—but seduction to what? To new roles in the world of comedy. The two sisters mock the old men as sheep. This conceit echoes and doubles the image of Nicobulus as the ram of Phrixus about to be sheared of its gold, which Chrysalus used early on (241-42). The Bacchides are suitable, if diminished, successors to the great Chrysalus as sheepherders. We know that the Bacchides' seduction has succeeded when the two *senes* accept their appellation of "sheep" (1140 *haec oves volunt vos*). Once they have imaginatively adopted this role, no matter whether they threaten to transform themselves into a more virile and fierce type of herd animal (1148), they are self-condemned to be led, not to lead. Though Nicobulus is slow to recognize the fact (he protests vigorously at 1163), this acceptance of role also implies submission to the (nontheatrical) seduction, and the two old men are finally drawn into the house.

The house of the Bacchides, as part of the fixed backdrop of the Roman stage, is a powerful presence in this play. The house swallows Pistoclerus at the beginning when the Bacchides seduce him into the role of lover.[33] Lydus the agelastic tutor reminds us of the theatrical presence of the house when he bursts from it and rants back at the door:

omnis ad perniciem instructa domus opime atque opipare.

(373)

This whole house is bounteously and beauteously bedecked for deviltry.

Into this house now vanish the two *senes*; this stage movement underscores the re-beginning of the play.[34]

The *Bacchides* is an excellent example of what Duckworth calls

[33] The house of the courtesan Phronesium is just such a devouring presence to the young Diniarchus in the *Truculentus*. Dinarchus speaks of the *"fores / quae opsorbent quidquid venit intra pessulos"* (350-51).

[34] There may even be a richer and more delightful irony. Lacey (1978-79) suggests that one reason for Plautus' suppression of Menander's father-son scene (see notes 2 and 3 above) may have been in order to double the roles of the fathers and sons. Thus the old men, whose voices the audience would likely recognize, repeat the roles of the sons at the beginning of the play. Phylogeny recapitulates ontongeny in a mordantly funny Plautine inversion.

the "duality method."[35] There are two *senes*, two *adulescentes*, and of course twin Bacchides. These pairs run in linear tandem through the play. The *Bacchides* is a double play in another sense, though, with the Chrysalus play nested inside the Bacchides play. Chrysalus comes late and leaves early. He is the playwright of the inner play, his command undisputed while he is on stage. The outer play is controlled by Bacchis.[36] The total play, then, is richly textured with the linear plots interwoven with the nested ones.

With the second seduction/induction completed and the renewal of the comic cycle firmly established, the play can close with a brief epilogue:

> Hi senes nisi fuissent nihili jam inde ab adulescentia,
> non hodie hoc tantum flagitium facerent canis capitibus;
> neque adeo haec faceremus, ni antehac vidissemus fieri
> ut apud lenones rivales filiis fierent patres.
> spectatores, vos valere volumus, [et] clare adplaudere.
>
> (1207-11)

> If these old men had not been worthless from their youth, today they wouldn't at their age have committed such a crime. Nor would we have acted these things, if we hadn't before now seen fathers become their sons' rivals in the brothels. Spectators, we wish for your health and your loud applause.

The form seems to imply a moral, but what is the moral? Plautus says he has given us an accurate picture of the age, but he does *not* claim that, by holding up a mirror to the age, his comedy corrects it.

This epilogue will not give us the usual moral or the message of the *Bacchides*. We are left to sort it out for ourselves. The *Bacchides* by its form acknowledges the seamless union of festival and theatre

---

[35] Duckworth (1952), 184-85.

[36] Bacchis and Chrysalus may have been played by the same actor. The voice would probably have been recognizable as that of the same player, no matter how well differentiated, thus supplying another ironic texture to this play. Though persuasive, this suggestion does not admit of proof.

that Segal discusses: to give oneself up to holiday license is to adopt a role (*amator*) or mask in the world of comedy. Both the *adulescentes* and the *senes* of this play do so.

Against this background the figure of Chrysalus stands as an enduring enigma. He too has a role to play (*servus callidus*), but he finally refuses to play it any longer. The clown will not stay and entertain us with his parodies of Roman triumphs and military honors. Chrysalus walks out of the world of comedy, and however joking his exit may seem, however well the renewal of the comic world through the second seduction/induction scene deemphasizes that exit, the fact that Chrysalus never returns must trouble us somewhat.

Plautus may have been as impatient with the restrictions of his genre and medium as Chrysalus is with the confines of his own play. From this impatience, then, may grow the far more sophisticated and metatheatrical structure of a play like the *Pseudolus*.

CHAPTER VII

Words, Words, Words

By a long tradition, the leader of a troupe of comedians has been the clown, the performer whose mask or make-up is the most glaring, who mimics or changes costume more than the others, who plays at playing and visibly reduplicates the act of acting. [1]
—Leo Salingar

It CAN scarce be construed an accident that the creators of *A Funny Thing Happened on the Way to the Forum* chose to call their hero Pseudolus. In the resurrection of the spirit of Plautine comedy, the shade of its greatest hero was bound to be reincarnated also. One of those rare heroes who live on outside their original work (like Falstaff and Alceste), Pseudolus has become the archetypal representation of one aspect of Plautus' creative genius.

It is therefore all the more curious that virtually nothing in the way of literary criticism of this play has appeared. Everyone seems to agree that it is marvelous, but no one is quite sure why.

The admirable exception is the recent article by John Wright, to which I am much indebted in the following pages. [2] Wright argues that the key to understanding Pseudolus' comic greatness lies in the power of Plautine language to transform him, to move him from a serious to a comic world with ever-increasing heroic stature, and finally to identify him with Plautus himself.

In what follows I shall retrace this development and argue for Pseudolus' own control of the transformational process. The *Pseudolus* is a microcosm of the development we have been following throughout this book, moving from Epidicus the improvisational player talking himself into the role of the *servus callidus* to Chrysalus in the *Bacchides*, an improvisational playwright too powerful to be contained any longer either by his role or his play. In the character of Pseudolus, a playwright who must eventually give up playing a

[1] Salingar (1974), 94.
[2] Wright (1975), 403-16.

role in his own creation, we reach the climax of this movement. Parallel to this conflict between the roles of player and playwright, I believe we can also trace in this play an underlying tension between the merely verbal and the theatrical, between text and artistic whole.

The play opens after a two-line prologue with a scene between Pseudolus and his young master Calidorus that centers, visually and verbally, on a letter (3-132). Its contents are secret at first: Calidorus, in great distress, has been carrying it about with him for several days but has refused to share its contents (9-10). After some twenty lines of building suspense, Calidorus hands over the letter to Pseudolus to read—and Pseudolus immediately makes a risqué joke about the handwriting:

> PS. ut opinor, quaerunt litterae hae sibi liberos;
>   alia aliam scandit.
> CALI.   ludis jam ludo tuo?   (23-24)

> PS. It seems to me the letters are trying to beget children; one climbs on top of another.
> CALI. Are you still playing your own game?

Indeed it takes nearly twenty lines of byplay before Pseudolus actually commences reading (41).

The letter, though often interrupted, functions as an internal prologue, providing us all the background details of the impending sale of Calidorus' *amica* to a Macedonian soldier of fortune. The numerous gags that interrupt this exposition are more than comic relief; they function as Pseudolus' assertion that the play is to be a comedy, not a tragedy. Note particularly lines 24: *ludis jam ludo tuo?* Pseudolus does not accept the play as handed to him in the letter (which functions also like a script or script outline). Already he insists on playing his own game with it, as he will throughout the play. Calidorus mourns his state in lines that can only be paratragic:

> quasi solstitialis herba paullisper fui:
> repente exortus sum, repentino occidi.   (38-39)

> Like the brief summer flower am I—swiftly grown up and so swiftly cut down.

Pseudolus' lack of sympathy with such tragic pretensions emerges quickly. He not only mocks the script he is handed in this scene, he criticizes it as well:

CALI. est misere scriptum, Pseudole.
PS.   oh! miserrume.
CALI. quin fles?
PS.   pumiceos oculos habeo: non queo
lacrumam exorare ut exspuant unam modo.
CALI. quid ita?
PS.   genu' nostrum semper siccoculum fuit.
CALI. nilne adjuvare me audes?
PS.   quid faciam tibi?
CALI. eheu!
PS.   'eheu'? id quidem hercle ne parsis: dabo.

(74-79)

CALI. It is a tale of woe, Pseudolus.
PS. O, most woeful!
CALI. Why don't you weep?
PS. My eyes are made of pumice; I can't squeeze one tear
  out of them.
CALI. How so?
PS. My family's always been a dry-eyed sort.
CALI. Won't you help me at all?
PS. What shall I do for you?
CALI. O, woe!
PS. "O, woe"? Heavens, don't stint yourself of those. I'll
  give you some.

Pseudolus goes on to mock Calidorus' mournful cry of "O, woe" at some length. Note the triple-edged irony of line 74, which we might translate "it is tragically written." Pseudolus' comment of course means that the handwriting itself is a tragedy, but I think it may also mean that the plot laid out for the play by this letter is a piece of hack writing. We shall soon have more evidence for Pseudolus as theatre critic. Pseudolus has no patience with cliché, as his reworking of proverbs and play with language shows (e.g., 123-

24), and he equally resists this stock New Comedy plot. Finally, though, he agrees to help, but note the phrasing:

> spero alicunde hodie me bona opera aut hac mea
> tibi inventurum esse auxilium argentarium.
> atque id futurum unde unde dicam nescio,
> nisi quia futurumst: ita supercilium salit.   (104-7)

I hope today by hook or crook to find some cash to comfort you. Where it's going to come from I can't say—except it will come. See how my eyebrow's twitching.

Regrettably, we have no proof that Pseudolus' mask had a mechanical eyebrow he could twitch at this point. Nonetheless, the phrase *ita supercilium salit* rivets our attention on the slave mask and the character that flows from the mask. In masked drama the mask itself energizes the performer, calls him into his role, and from that role flows the action of the play. Pseudolus, the *servus callidus*, as his mask shows him to be, is now aroused and in action. His mask tells him so.

Like a typical *servus callidus*, Pseudolus' first thought is to tackle Calidorus' father Simo for the money, the traditional court of first resort, but he goes far beyond that. He faces the audience and addresses them in the guise of a magistrate speaking before a *contio*:

> nunc, ne quis dictum sibi neget, dico omnibus,
> pube praesenti in contione, omni poplo,
> omnibus amicis notisque edico meis
> in hunc diem a me ut caveant, ne credant mihi.   (125-28)

Now, to prevent any later denial, I say to you all, to all the men in the assembly, to all the people, to all my friends and acquaintances I declare this day: beware of me! don't trust me!

Pseudolus warns the audience not to trust him, for he may even trick them.

Pseudolus' challenge is even bolder than it may seem. His is a conjurer's challenge: with nothing up his sleeves, Pseudolus dares the audience not to trust him, and then goes right ahead and traps their imagination with his.

This bold challenge is needed to establish Pseudolus' claim to the stage, for a doughty champion comes to dispute possession with him: Ballio. Indeed, to judge from later performance history (long after the non-illusory vitality of Plautine theatre was sapped by over-large stone theatres), Ballio could easily win the contest. When Roscius was an actor in Rome, his bravura performance was as Ballio, not Pseudolus.[3] His entrance is one of the strongest in all Roman comedy. Singing the exultantly sadistic strains of a Plautine *canticum*,[4] Ballio arrives cracking his whip. The one instance where we may certainly infer Ballio's use of the whip shows something of the vocal and emotional range of the part. Ballio begins with mock sympathy, perhaps even a soothing gesture—and then strikes again on *em*:

quid nunc? doletne? em sic datur. . . .   (155)

What now? Does it hurt? There, take *that*!

Ballio enters in the center of a mass of cowering slaves; he is the center of action, the star. He is celebrating his birthday (179) with an orgy of language that, as Wright has pointed out, transforms him from pimp to a tragic tyrant:[5]

lenone ex Ballione regem Iasonem.   (193)

. . . from the pimp Ballio to king Jason.

And then—after sixty lines—Calidorus and Pseudolus break

---

[3] Cicero, *Pro Q. Roscio comoedo* 7.20. Garton (1972), 169-88, gives a fascinating interpretation of how Roscius might have acted the part of Ballio. He sees Ballio as the apotheosis of the *leno*, and suggests that this is what attracted Roscius to this part, rather than the title role. I offer my own suggestion below for the prominence of the role of Ballio in the changed playing conditions of the late Republic.

[4] Thoroughly Plautine, says Fraenkel (1960), 136-42.

[5] Wright (1975), 407.

free from Ballio's spell and begin to discuss his performance.[6] Calidorus is impressed: he describes it with a familiar acting-style word, *magnufice* (194). Olympio in the *Casina* approaches his master *magnufice* (723). Sagaristio spits *magnufice* (308) in the *Persa* in the scene where, laden with the money pouch, he attempts to steal the limelight from Toxilus. Even more significantly, the adverb will next be used in this play by Pseudolus himself before he launches into a send-up of the tragic style (702). All of these situations involve adoption of a role—and usually a stock or parody role. More importantly, the roles often do not work, as in *Casina* and *Persa*.[7] It is a challenge phrased as faint praise: Ballio's acting is grand, though not necessarily good.

We are reminded that Ballio's *canticum* is a performance by the form of the scene as well: an eavesdropping scene. The structure of such a scene not only imparts a power to the eavesdroppers (that of superior knowledge) but also aligns the eavesdroppers with the audience: we are both audiences. Their very invisibility (to Ballio) gives Calidorus and Pseudolus a power that the verbal texture of the scene might seem to deny. We see Ballio through Pseudolus' eyes: Ballio is *maleficus* (194) and a *pestis* (204).

As Ballio falls temporarily silent, the two eavesdroppers discuss what they have learned. Pseudolus promises aid again (232). In an interestingly self-conscious passage, Calidorus must beg Pseudolus for permission to adopt the *adulescens amans* role. His justification?— all the fun lies therein.

> non jucundumst nisi amans facit stulte. (238)

> It's no fun unless the lover plays the fool.

Like an out-of-work actor, however, he soon agrees to play whatever part Pseudolus assigns to him:

---

[6] I believe Plautus emphasizes the interruption by beginning it in the middle of a line, but it would require a statistical study to prove this.

[7] The exception is Pseudolus' own creation, Simia, who behaves *magnufice* (911) and still gets away with it. Even there, though, there is still a tinge of criticism to Pseudolus' comment on Simia's acting style.

mane, mane, jam ut voles med esse ita ero. (240)

Wait, wait, I'll be whatever you want me to.

As we shall see in the course of the play, this is no stray motif. Pseudolus the poet will virtually write Calidorus out of the script.

Pseudolus and Calidorus now accost the slave-dealer in a scene (243-393) which has troubled many critics, since the two seem not to know that Ballio has made arrangements to sell Calidorus' mistress.[8] Yet surely Wright is correct in asserting that the two only feign ignorance,[9] no challenge at all for the protean player Pseudolus will soon prove himself to be. If we need further proof that the two are role-playing here, we need look only at Pseudolus' indignation when Ballio suggests a possible source of money:

surruperet hic patri, audacissime?[10] (288)

He should steal it from his father, you scoundrel?

The pretended ignorance of the two is merely part of their attempt to appeal to Ballio's nonexistent better feelings.

The famous *flagitatio* scene in which Calidorus and Pseudolus heap insults on Ballio has been universally admired and its antecedents in Italian folk justice duly noted and traced.[11] Note, however, that it is Ballio, not Pseudolus, who controls the scene—despite that fact that in the confrontation Calidorus and Pseudolus are two to one, a strong working majority.[12] The staging deliberately undercuts the two accusers: standing on either side of the *leno*, they form a

---

[8] E.g., Williams (1956), 429, where he insists the two must not know, since their "guilt" sets the atmosphere of the scene. Guilt seems singularly inappropriate in any dealings with the pimp, who, as old Simo says, deserves to be cheated whenever possible (1225). Simo proceeds to practice what he preaches.

[9] Wright (1975), 409, n. 11.

[10] Calidorus is less secure as a role-player. He candidly admits it would be difficult to steal from so sharp an old man as Simo (290). He then recovers himself (perhaps at a warning signal from Pseudolus), and mutters something about *pietas* forbidding such an action (291).

[11] See Wright (1975), 409 and n. 13 with references.

[12] Cf. Wright (1975), 409.

triangle whose apex of power is Ballio. Yes, the *flagitatio* scene leaves Ballio still in control—but *flagitatio* was not Pseudolus' idea. Calidorus takes the lead and orders Pseudolus to join him in this verbal assault:

> Pseudole, adsiste altrim secus atque onera hunc maledictis.
>
> (357)

> Pseudolus, step up and load this man with curses!

His bid to resolve the situation, entertaining as it may be as theatre, fails, and after Ballio's triumphant exit, he must turn to his slave for orders (383 *ecquid imperas?*).

Pseudolus responds with a war cry as powerful yet vague as the promises that he made preceding Ballio's entrance:

> illic homo meus est, nisi omnes di me atque homines
>   deserunt.
> exossabo ego illum simulter itidem ut murenam coquos.
>
> (381-82)

> The man is mine, unless all the gods and men desert me. I'll debone him, just as a cook does an eel.

> hoc ego oppidum admoenire, ut hodie capiatur, volo.   (384)

> I want to besiege this city and take it today.

The familiar military and siege metaphors of the *servus callidus* appear. A typical plot is underway, and it includes the need for another person (385), whom Calidorus will provide. Pseudolus will give no details, however, for a wonderfully metatheatrical reason:

> nolo bis iterari, sat sic longae fiunt fabulae.   (388)

> I don't want to repeat it twice; plays are long enough as it is.[13]

---

[13] Cf. *Mercator* 1007 and *Poenulus* 1224.

Pseudolus' "poet" soliloquy that now follows addresses the problem the preceding scene has set. Words alone as weapons have failed. Ballio is too ruthless and intelligent to be cowed by Calidorus' words in the *flagitatio* scene. We must advance a level, from words to webs of words, to the level of plots and dramatic poetry. Pseudolus now becomes a poet who weaves those lying plots that exist nowhere in the world but in the theatre of his own mind:

Postquam illic hinc abiit, tu astas solus, Pseudole.
quid nunc acturu's, postquam erili filio
largitu's dictis dapsilis? ubi sunt ea?
quoi neque paratast gutta certi consili
neque adeo argenti neque—nunc quid faciam scio.
neque exordiri primum unde occipias habes.
neque ad detexundam telam certos terminos.
sed quasi poeta, tabulas quom cepit sibi,
quaerit quod nusquam gentiumst, reperit tamen,
facit illud veri simile quod mendacium est,
nunc ego poeta fiam: viginti minas,
quae nunc nusquam sunt gentium, inveniam tamen.

(394-405)

Now that he's gone you stand alone, Pseudolus. What are
you going to do, now that you've stuffed the young master
with a banquet of words? Where are they now? You don't
have a drop of definite plan or any money or—
(Now I know what I'll do.)
You don't have a place to start nor a definite goal for
weaving your plot.
(But like a poet, when he takes pen in hand, seeking what
exists nowhere on earth, yet finding it, makes a lie seem very
truth, now I'll become a poet. Those twenty minae, which
now are nowhere on earth, I'll find all the same.)

Just like Epidicus in the monologue at the beginning of his play
(*Epidicus* 81-101), Pseudolus here must talk himself into his role—
the role of playwright. We see again the structure of two voices
within the soliloquy, one accusing and doubting, the other voice of

the role already assumed. Pseudolus begins in doubt and gloom. He has filled Calidorus with words, but what are words? *Where* are they, once spoken? Pseudolus needs more than words, he needs poetry and the power of its truth-seeming fictions. He needs the power of dramatic poetry, of the theatrical.

Another eavesdropping scene follows (415-573), in which Pseudolus overhears the *senex* Simo and his friend Callipho talking. Pseudolus is presented with both information and a challenge: Simo suspects his son's affair but has been concealing his knowledge (422 *dissimulabam*). Whatever Pseudolus' first line of attack was, he now drops it, as he tells us: 423 *occisa est haec res*. His succeeding asides (435, 443-44) endorse the views of Callipho, who counsels leniency to his friend Simo. As usual Pseudolus' interjections are meant to interpret the scene for us, but his second aside is so enthusiastic and loud that it betrays his presence:

> *O Zeu, ⟨Zeu⟩ quam pauci estis homines commodi! em,*
> illic est pater patrem esse ut aequomst filio.[14]　　(443-44)

> O, Zeus, Zeus, how rare good fellows are! There, that's the sort of father a boy ought to have.

Plautus reminds us of the theatricality of Pseudolus' entrance into the scene in two ways. First, Pseudolus instructs himself to get a speech ready (and for what purpose):

> . . . itur ad te, Pseudole.
> orationem tibi para advorsum senem.　　(453-54)

> It's up to you Pseudolus. Get yourself a speech ready for the old man.

Then Pseudolus enters and strikes an attitude, which Simo comments on:

> statum vide hominis, Callipho, quam basilicum!　　(458)

---

[14] The appeal to Zeus, especially since it is in Greek, hints at paratragedy. Pseudolus' theatricality may be what betrays him here.

Look at the man's pose, Callipho, how regal!

Basilicum and its related adjective *basilice* are again acting-style words,[15] comparable to *magnufice* and *graphice*.

In this scene Pseudolus adopts two roles which illustrate the power of words, but it is his acting, his adoption of role, that makes them come alive. Simo himself acknowledges the power of Pseudolus' words to make him a Socrates, when he warns Callipho:

> conficiet jam te hic verbis ut tu censeas
> non Pseudolum, sed Socratem tecum loqui.   (464-65)

> He'll so confound you with words that you'll think you're
> talking not with Pseudolus, but Socrates.

It seems scarcely necessary to expatiate on the implied power to transform the appearance of things by words involved in this characterization. Pseudolus adopts a character with even more dangerous resonances to it: he becomes the Delphic oracle whose words men interpret at their own peril:

> . . . si quid vis roga.
> quod scibo Delphis tibi responsum dicito.   (479-80)

> Ask what you will. I'll tell you what I know in Delphic
> utterance.

Simo is all too eager to rush in with interpretation.

Pseudolus grows angry with Sino's mockery of his acting and with his general treatment. He loses his temper, and in a fit of bravado warns Simo not to trust him, for he intends to extract some money from Simo this day:

> praedico ut caveas, dico, inquam, ut caveas. cave.   (517)

---

[15] Cf. *Persa* 462, where Sagaristio enters in costume as the Persian. *Agitur* and *statur* in 457 also have a theatrical undertone.

I forewarn you to beware. I warn you, I say, to beware.
Beware!

Cave echoes the *caveant* of Pseudolus' earlier warning to us in the
audience (128). Simo becomes an audience here for Pseudolus' poetic
creation and, what is more, a paying audience.

Pseudolus and Simo make two wagers on the success of Pseudolus' efforts: one on Pseudolus' ability to get money from a fore-
warned Simo, the second on Pseudolus' ability to steal young Calidorus' mistress from Ballio. Simo is absolutely certain that, now
his suspicions are aroused, Pseudolus cannot possibly get money out
of him under any circumstances (504-5, *non potest / argentum auferri
. . .*). Pseudolus takes up the challenge:

> numquam edepol quoiquam supplicabo, dum quidem
> tu ⟨vivos⟩ vives. tu mi hercle argentum dabis,
> aps te equidem sumam. (507-9)

As long as you still live and breathe, I'll beg from no one
else. I swear you'll give me cash: I'll certainly relieve you of
it.

Pseudolus mocks the old man's proclaimed wariness (516 *cavere*)
by thrice crying beware (517). Pseudolus caps the first section of
his challenge with a joke that artfully disguises a transition:

> PS. servitum tibi me abducito, ni fecero.
> SIMO. bene atque amice dicis. nam nunc non meu's
> (520-21)

PS. Make me your slave, if I fail.
SIMO. That's nice and friendly, for of course you're not my
slave now.

The joke of a man wearing a slave mask saying "make me your
slave if I fail" should be obvious. Simo's line adds a special irony:
who belongs to whom? Simo thinks he owns Pseudolus, but it is
really Pseudolus who owns the play and its characters. Recall 381:
illic homo meus est.

Pseudolus has in fact committed himself to a wager that is on the face of it impossible. An expert at both shortchange and quick-change, he now succeeds in inducing Simo to alter the bet. He seems to propose to do something even more difficult than gulling Simo; he proposes to steal the girl from Ballio *per doctos dolos* (527). He converts Simo's incredulity at this claim into a further bet on the outcome of this action (526-46). Simo will now give Pseudolus twenty *minae* if he succeeds in stealing the girl from the pimp; this done, Pseudolus will have fulfilled the terms of the first bet.[16]

At the very last moment Simo suspects a conspiracy (540 *consutis dolis*) that Pseudolus fervently and artfully denies in Delphic words:

> si sumu' compecti seu consilium umquam iniimus
> aut si de istac re umquam inter nos convenimus,
> quasi in libro quom scribuntur calamo litterae,
> stilis me totum usque ulmeis conscribito.   (543-45)

If we've ever conspired together or embarked on any plot or
ever agreed among ourselves about this matter, as when
letters are written by pen in a book, then write me black and
blue with your elm-wood pen.

Line 544a is utterly essential to this Delphic utterance;[17] there is no written (*scribuntur calamo litterae*) plot, but only the one Pseudolus will improvise.

After an inordinately long and possibly confusing induction, the play can at last begin. Simo and Callipho both speak of the *ludi* that Pseudolus will now provide them:

> SIMO. indice ludos nunciam. . . .   (546)

Proclaim the games now.

---

[16] Williams (1956), 434-40, is much concerned by the interrelations of the two wagers and argues that their present state is the Plautine reordering. It is important to realize, however, that the text is perfectly playable as is. The ambiguity of the relation between the two wagers is intended. Simo does not quite realize to what he has assented. Pseudolus knows precisely.

[17] This is wrongly deleted by Leo (and Ussing before him).

CALI. lubidost ludos spectare, Pseudole. (552)

It would be a pleasure to see your games, Pseudolus.

Pseudolus now orders them to leave

. . . date locum fallaciis . . . (558)

Give way for the gimmicks . . .

in what seems to be a technical term for quitting the stage, for in Pseudolus' ensuing soliloquy he argues that those who cannot provide novel plays should quit the stage in favor of those who can:

. . . det locum. . . . (570)

. . . let him give way. . . .

Pseudolus' ensuing soliloquy (562-73) is his first formal direct address to the audience (note the *vos* in line 562):

suspicio est mi nunc vos suspicarier,
me idcirco haec tanta facinora promittere,
qui vos oblectem, hanc fabulam dum transigam,
neque sim facturus quod facturum dixeram. (562-65)

Now I suspect that you suspect I promised such great deeds just now just to divert you, while I was performing the play, and that I'm not going to do what I said I would.

Notice the deliciously emphatic motif of distrust in 562: "I suspect that you suspect. . . ." Pseudolus has warned us all not to trust him (128), and believes now we may think all his boasts of the previous scene to have been puffery for the sake of the play's amusement value (564).[18] He is standing outside any illusionistic space at the

---

[18] Just the sort of puffery any good prologue engages in; for example, cf. the prologue to the *Captivi* 53ff.

moment, but paradoxically his assertions seem charged with more fervor, more weight, and more "reality." He does not know *how* he will accomplish his purpose, only that he will do it (567-68).

While the flute-player fills the intermission (573a),[19] let us pause and reflect on what we have seen up till now. We have seen the typical New Comedy dilemma handed to Pseudolus as a script in the form of a letter. We have seen Calidorus' idea, the use of the force of mere words (the *flagitatio* scene) also fail. Even Pseudolus' first idea, to defraud Simo of the necessary money, seems to have failed, because the old man has somehow gotten wind of the plot (420-22). And yet Pseudolus has left us with assurances that he will bring it all off and will return in a few moments singing a victory *canticum*. We must admire Pseudolus for his consummate self-confidence, if nothing else.

His *canticum* on returning to the stage (574-93) outlines the sequence of the rest of the plot, just in case we did not catch it the first time around: first he will attack Ballio, then the old man (585-86). Note that at the crucial juncture between the two plot elements he appeals for the attention and participation of the audience, a direct imperative appeal: 585, *date operam modo*. Pseudolus knows the audience must be even more alert than usual to follow his double, even triple, plotting (580 *duplicis, triplicis dolos*).

Suddenly the play is thrown into flux again by the arrival of Harpax, servant to the Macedonian captain (594-666). We will never know the nature of Pseudolus' original plan to steal the girl from Ballio, for, with a swift warning to the audience (600 *st! tace, tace*),[20] Pseudolus announces he must improvise a new scheme using this gift from heaven of the letter and the token that Harpax carries; his previous plans must be discarded:

[19] This is one of the few places to our knowledge where such an intermission occurs. Pseudolus calls attention to the flute-player once again to emphasize the theatricality of his actions. Just so, in the *Stichus* 713 and 760 a joke is made of offering the flute-player a drink. When the revellers succeed in inducing him to join them in a drink, the fiction of the stage has conquered the realities of performance—and the onstage revelry seems therefore all the more "real."

[20] Note that the audience is here treated just like another actor/eavesdropper. Cf. Calidorus (207 *vah! tace*) and Pseudolus (195 *sed tace. . . .*) in their eavesdropping scene.

st! tace, tace, meus hic est homo, ni omnes di atque homines
    deserunt.
novo consilio nunc mi opus est,
nova res haec subito mi objectast: (600-2)

Shush! Softly, softly—the man is mine, unless all the gods
and men desert me. I need a new plan now; this new
situation has been suddenly thrust upon me.

Pseudolus' ability to adopt the role of Surus, Ballio's slave,
easily wins for him the letter and the token from Harpax.[21] Pseudolus
cleverly concentrates his efforts on attempting to get the balance of
money from Harpax, which only increases his resistance. By contrast
he gives up the letter and token unprompted—yet these in a sense
have a value of fifteen *minae*, far more than the five he carries in
cash.

Pseudolus' exultant soliloquy after Harpax' departure, like the
first scene, has a letter for visual and verbal center:

namque ipsa Opportunitas non potuit mi opportunius
advenire quam haec allatast mi opportune epistula.
nam haec allata cornu copiaest, ubi inest quidquid volo:
hic doli, hic fallaciae omnes, hic sunt sycophantiae,
hic argentum, hic amica amanti erili filio.   (669-73)

Opportunity herself couldn't have come more opportunely to
me than this opportune letter just arrived. Here's my
cornucopia, with anything I want in it. Here are schemes,
here are all my tricks, here are treacheries, here's money,
and here's a mistress for my loving young master.

The situation parallels the first scene in other ways, too. Pseudolus
has been handed a text (in this case not a complete plot, but the
source of one). He can improvise whatever he likes from this bare

---

[21] There is even room for Pseudolus to make some specific gesture or movement to indicate his adoption of the role. Surus may be the effeminate, pathic
slave type. Something of the sort is implied by the joke in 607 that he is a
"Subballio."

verbal material (672 *hic doli, hic fallaciae omnes*). By improvisation he can now in fact weave a triple delusion (691 *tris deludam*).

Inspired by his dramatic success in the role of Surus, Pseudolus greets the returning Calidorus and his friend Charinus in a self-conscious parody of tragic style:

> PS. magnufice hominem compellabo.
> CALI.   quoia vox resonat?
> PS.   io!
>   io te, te, turanne, te, te ego, qui imperitas Pseudolo,
>   quaero quoi ter trina triplicia, tribu' modis tria gaudia,
>   artibus tribu' tris demeritas dem laetitias, de tribus
>   fraude partas per malitiam, per dolum et fallacias;
>   in libello hoc opsignato ad te attuli pauxillulo.   (702-6)

> PS. Grandiosely shall I address the man.
> CALI. What voice re-echoes?
> PS. Hail, hail to thee, thee, my lord, thee, who lordest
>   over Pseudolus, I seek, to give thee thrice threefold triple
>   news: three joys three ways, triply deserved delights in
>   threefold fashion, from three men fiendishly defrauded, by
>   hook and crook, in this minuscule missive sealed up I bring
>   to thee.

Note Pseudolus' comment on his own theatrical style: *magnufice*. A victory achieved through theatricality (the deception of Harpax) can only be celebrated through theatricality (the paratragedy). Pseudolus also knows, however, not to overstay his welcome on stage and will not repeat what the audience already knows:

> horum caussa haec agitur spectatorum fabula;
> hi sciunt qui hic adfuerunt; vobis post narravero.   (720-21)

> This play's being performed for the benefit of the spectators.
> They know what's gone before; I'll tell you later.

One item of business remains. Now that the plot has changed (once? twice? we can hardly say at this point), the first helper Pseudolus asked for, who has arrived in the person of Charinus, will not do. He needs a sharp actor, and that means a slave (728). Pseudolus will indeed become a poet, because he will provide a plot (the letter), a costume (751 *exornavero*), props (the token), and plenty of stage directions (764 *onerabo meis praeceptis*). As Pseudolus says, there you have the whole play: 754 *em tibi omnem fabulam.*[22] Pseudolus now disappears for nearly one-hundred-fifty lines, yielding the stage to Ballio. Ballio himself is preceded by a *puer* (767-89), whose abject fear of the *leno* would seem to presage a bravura scene for the terrible Ballio to top his great first *canticum*. Comically, though, we find the great Ballio overturned by a mere cook and, as Wright noted, solely through the power of words.[23]

But are they only words? The insults of Calidorus and Pseudolus were mere words, insults that could not harm the great Ballio. The words of the cook are of a higher order: they are mythic. This *coquos gloriosus* (see 794) begins with a catalogue song (814ff.) of condiments that simply revels in verbal virtuosity. Soon, however, mythic allusions begin to embellish his boasting: the cattle of Neptune (834) and Jupiter, who dines on the odors the cook sends heavenward (840-46). Eventually, the cook proposes to play Medea to Ballio's Pelias and rejuvenate him through his cooking.

The cook's mythic language represents a middle ground or transitional stage between the merely verbal at the beginning of this play and the theatrical at the end. The cook is not yet capable of complete dramatic self-creation; his theatrical thinking is parodistic, borrowing earlier forms (the Medea story) and converting them to his own purpose. His words, though, do have dramatic power, and with them he frightens the great Ballio. This points the way to the resolution of the play through Pseudolus' dramatic activity.

Certainly while the cook is on stage Pseudolus cannot be far from our minds for several reasons. It is entirely possible, for example, that Pseudolus and the cook were played by the same actor. Given the difficulty of disguising the voice behind the mask, Plautus

---

[22] See Wright (1975), 413-14, for a more succinct summary than mine. We shall see below, though, some cause to avoid his characterization of Pseudolus as a theatrical director, an anachronistic view of his role that conceals some of the functioning of the creative process.

[23] Wright (1975), 405-6.

may have thus subliminally pointed for his audience the parallel between the two. The cook's mere opposition to Ballio in the scene also pairs him with Pseudolus. Even Ballio's mind seems to grasp the connection, for after the cook's exit the warnings of Simo begin to hit home for Ballio (892-904). Indeed, Ballio's use of *cavere* (898) may draw us back to Pseudolus at 128. Ballio meditates fearfully on what schemes (902 *dolis*) Pseudolus may have been concocting. Ballio's exit line, which once again recalls us to Pseudolus' warning at 125-28, closes with Pseudolus' name as the very last word, preparing the way for Pseudolus' entrance:

> profecto ne quis quicquam credat Pseudolo.　　　　　(904)

> . . . to make sure no one trusts Pseudolus an inch.

The subtle interplay of theatrical creator (Pseudolus) and creation (Simia) in the following scene is worth studying in some detail (905-55). Note that this is by no means a typical Plautine plotter's scene. There are other scenes in which the *servus callidus* rehearses another character in a part, but this resembles none of them. Pseudolus enters delivering a soliloquy—which suddenly turns out not to be a soliloquy. The first two lines could easily open a soliloquy, but when he arrives at the *te* in line 907 we realize that Pseudolus is talking to an absent auditor. Pseudolus realizes it only a line later with a line that subtly mocks the convention of self-addressed soliloquy:

> sed ubi illic est? sumne ego homo insipiens, qui haec mecum
> 　　　　　egomet loquar solus?　　　　　(908)

> But where is he? Am I some sort of fool, to soliloquize to myself?

Within the scene the lines function to underscore boldly the fact that Pseudolus himself will not peform the trick. He needs another actor, Simia, who is accorded a strong entrance that emphasizes his similarity to his creator Pseudolus. Pseudolus greets him with:

136

ut it, ut magnufice infert sese! (911)

How he advances, how grandiose his carriage!

We remember how Simo greeted Pseudolus with comments on his acting style (458).

Simia, as Pseudolus' creation, is even more of a comic slave than Pseudolus himself is—and he is a consciously theatrical one. His type would be instantly established by his mask. His very first line speaks of his proper (stock) role:

fuit meum officium ut facerem, fateor. (913)

That was my part to play, I admit.

He is rude to his master/creator and will not take blocking (i.e., stage movement directions):

> PS. ambula ergo cito.
> SIMIA.   immo otiose volo.   (920)

> PS. Walk faster, then.
> SIMIA. I prefer a leisurely pace.

He even refuses rewards for his labors, as a good comic slave should:

> PS. sed ego quae tibi bona dabo et faciam si hanc sobrie
>   rem accurassis!
> SIMIA. potin ut taceas?   (939-40)

> PS. What marvelous gifts I'll award and grant you,
> if you manage this scheme sensibly!
> SIMIA. Can't you keep quiet?

Most importantly, Simia insists on his own creative, improvisatory contributions to Pseudolus' play. He boasts of his powers, but refuses to specify his course of action when Pseudolus asks him about it.

We are only promised something on the order of the Mercury/Sosia
scene from the *Amphitruo*:

> numquam edepol erit ill' potior Harpax quam ego. habe
>   animum bonum:
> pulchre ego hanc explicatam tibi rem dabo.
> sic ego illum dolis atque mendaciis
> in timorem dabo militarem advenam,
> ipsus sese ut neget esse eum qui siet
> meque ut esse autumet qui ipsus est.   (925-30)

That fellow will never be a better Harpax than I—cheer up!
I'll tie this situation into beautiful knots for you. I'll terrify
this foreign adventurer with so many schemes and lies that
he'll deny his own identity and admit that I am he himself.[24]

Simia challenges Pseudolus on his own ground, in the theatrical
kingdom of schemes and lies:

> te quoque etiam dolis atque mendaciis,
> qui magister es, antidibo, ut scias.   (932-33)

And I'll surpass even you my master in schemes and lies, as
you well know.

This challenge, so boldly stated, is suppressed by a truce when
Ballio returns to the stage (956). Pseudolus tells Simia that he is
on, and for once Simia agrees: 958 *tecum sentio*. Simia obviously
knows Toxilus' trick in the *Persa* of the soliloquy meant to be
overheard, and he uses it to catch Ballio's ear (960-62).[25] The scene
that ensues is a typical deception, thoroughly enlivened by the pres-

---

[24] A very real threat, for this is just what Mercury does to the hapless Sosia
in *Amphitruo* 331-462. In the theatre of role-playing it is a real comic possibility
that a more powerful player may steal the role and therefore the identity of a
less powerful player. Sosia jokes early on in their confrontations that Mercury
cannot be referring to him, because he speaks of *nescioquis* (331-32). By the
end of the scene, however, his is indeed a *nescioquis*, having lost his name and
appearance to the interloper.

[25] Just as Milphidippa does in the *Miles* 994-98.

ence of Pseudolus as commentator. Wright says Pseudolus functions as a theatrical director in the scene,[26] but he seems actually more the writer with first-night jitters. From his position as eavesdropper, Pseudolus mediates between the action and the audience and becomes an onstage audience himself. His asides subtly point the similarities between Simia and himself. When he comments on Simia's philosophizing (974), we are reminded that Pseudolus was himself such a philosopher earlier in the play: Socrates (465).

Simia's first crisis furthers the similarity. It is in fact the result of a failure of Pseudolus. Pseudolus has neglected to tell Simia (and *us*) the name of the Macedonian captain, but after some hesitation Simia improvises his way out of the embarrassment (984-91).[27] Ballio finally reads the letter to us (998-1014), and in the process becomes an actor manipulated through his lines. Note, however, that, unlike Dordalus reading Toxilus' forged letter in the *Persa*, Ballio is manipulated by an original, unaltered text (it is after all a real letter from the Macedonian captain). By putting it in a new context, however, i.e., in the hands of Simia, Pseudolus has made it part of his own play.[28]

Pseudolus is now left alone on stage with his fears (1017-37)— triple fears at that (1024 *triplici modo*). Even Pseudolus' fears must be one order better than usual. Pseudolus may have good grounds for fear: there is a theatrical hyperenergy about Simia, evidenced in the high-speed improvisation of his scene with Ballio. He is too peremptory even to spare time for a greeting (968-69), which indeed fits in with his military role, and always seems to be rushing (933 *propera*, 1016 *uter remorantur?*). Part of Pseudolus' fear must also be based on the similarities between Simia and himself. Simia has a similar acting style, taste for philosophizing, and gift for improvisation. If Simia has similar morals, Pseudolus' fears of betrayal

[26] Wright (1975), 414.

[27] Wright (1975), 414, assumes that Simia has only forgotten his lines. However, *nescit* here should mean "is ignorant of." I cannot parallel its use as a synonym for "to forget." This is more than a petty philological point, since the responsibility for the crisis depends on whether or not Pseudolus ever told Simia the name. Here Pseudolus' failure is made the basis for an impressive display of Simia's improvisational powers.

[28] Just as Plautus makes even the bits of text he seems merely to translate his own, as in the case of some of the fragments of the *Dis Exapaton*.

could come true (1019-22). Pseudolus' fears prove vain as Simia returns with the girl in tow, and all three, with Pseudolus in the lead, go off in triumph. After this Simia disappears totally from the play.

The play is not yet over, though, for we have yet to see the overthrow of Ballio demonstrated. Ballio returns to the stage exulting that, with the girl finally sold, he is safe from Pseudolus at last and looks forward to laughing at him: 1059 *nunc deridebo*. Ballio is of course mistaken: he is not the audience but the spectacle in this play.

Simo's entrance line only underscores this:

> visso quid rerum meus Ulixes egerit,
> jamne habeat signum ex arce Balliona. (1063-64)

> I'll see what my Ulysses has accomplished, whether he now has the statue from the Ballonian citadel.

His Ulysses is Pseudolus. The reference is to the theft of the Palladium, which, like other deeds of Ulysses, presumably had a background in south Italian theatre. The image is also exploited by Plautus in the great Trojan War *canticum* of Chrysalus in the *Bacchides*. Simo is coming to see how his own Chrysalus is getting on. Simo determines that Ballio and Pseudolus have met and enquires what has happened in an exchange that boldly underscores the verbal:

> SIMO. quid ait? quid narrat? quaeso, quid dicit tibi?
> BA. nugas theatri, verba quae in comoediis
>   solent lenoni dici, quae pueri sciunt:
>   malum et scelestum et peiiurum aibat esse me.
>   (1080-83)

> SIMO. What did he say? What was the story? I ask you, what did he tell you?
> BA. Theatrical nonsense, the usual things said to a pimp in comedies, the words the little boys know. He called me a scoundrel, a criminal, and a liar.

Both Simo and Ballio think of speech as mere words. It does not

matter to Ballio that the words are theatre words, for he has proved
himself a word master in the *flagitatio* scene. We must also not miss
the implication—that Pseudolus' words are trite, stock repetitions.
Ballio fails to recognize Pseudolus' originality. Theatre words have
more power than Ballio recognizes. They are animated by imagination, which is just what Ballio and Simo lack. Ballio sums up his
confidence this way:

> epistula atque imago me certum facit.　　　　　　　(1097)

> The letter and the seal image made me certain.

Yet what is theatre but word and image? Pseudolus has taken words,
the words of others in the form of letters, and made them into his
own play through his command of theatricality.

The original Harpax now returns to unravel the tidy but false
confidence of Ballio and Simo. Harpax enters soliloquizing on the
virtues of the faithful slave, enough in this comic world to label
him as much a fool as Ballio and Simo. Indeed the follies multiply
geometrically along with mistaken identities. First Ballio overhears
Harpax looking for a *leno* and a woman and therefore assumes
Harpax is an ordinary customer. Harpax then mistakes Simo for
the pimp.[29] Ironically, Ballio and Simo mistake Harpax for an
impostor hired by Pseudolus in an attempt to steal the girl.

When Ballio mistakes Harpax for a hireling of Pseudolus, he
and Simo are in such playful high spirits that they decide to try
their hands at play-making—with Harpax the victim.

> BA. . . . quid nunc mihi es auctor, Simo?
> SIMO. exploratorem hunc faciamus ludos suppositicum
> 　　　　adeo donicum ipsus sese ludo fieri senserit.
> 　　　　　　　　　　　　　　　　　　　(1166-68)

> BA. What plot do you suggest, Simo?
> SIMO. Let's try and impose on this impostor until he
> realizes he's being made a fool of.

---

[29] This mistake is all the more hilarious when one considers how far the
pimp's mask would differ from that of the *senex*.

Their playwriting, though, shows impoverished artistry and imagination: it is no more than a series of insults, obscene and otherwise, not even up to the level of the *flagitatio* scene. The truth is soon out, and the would-be playwrights exposed as mere players in Pseudolus' drama. Ballio must pay back Harpax' money and the money he foolishly promised to Simo. He then slinks away, never to reappear.

Simo surprises us. In a speech to the audience he tells us that he will not behave as the *senex* in comedy usually does:

> nunc mi certum est alio pacto Pseudolo insidias dare
> quam in aliis comoediis fit. . . .   (1239-40)

> Now I've decided to entrap Pseudolus in another way than
> the usual one in comedies. . . .

> superavit dolum Trojanum atque Ulixem Pseudolus.   (1244)

> Pseudolus has outdone Ulysses and that Trojan trick.

At the beginning of the scene Simo originally linked Pseudolus to Ulysses and thereby to Chrysalus in the *Bacchides*. Now he proclaims that Pseudolus has outdone them both.

Pseudolus returns, gloriously drunk, after Simo withdraws. He has been enjoying the rewards of wine and women that he once promised to Simia—but there is room for only one hero at the end of the play, and it is Pseudolus. Pseudolus has been dancing for the entertainment of Calidorus inside, and repeats some of his dance routine for us. His performance indoors ended somewhat ingloriously:

> ubi circumvortor, cado:
> id fuit naenia ludo.   (1278-78a)

> While I was pirouetting, I fell; that was the end of the
> dance.

Simo comes forth in answer to Pseudolus' cries to pay him the money owed under the bet. Simo makes two last attempts, both in theatrical modes, to recover his money. He tries paratragedy to stir Pseudolus' pity (1318-20), but Pseudolus has none, no more than he did for Calidorus' cries of *eheu* in the first scene (79-82). A brief return to the threatening *senex* role fails likewise (1325). Pseudolus will not be frightened. Theatre is Pseudolus' own game, and he cannot be beaten at it. Simo tries to leave, but Pseudolus will not let him. He is moving Simo about in this last scene, manipulating Simo like an actor in a play. He insists Simo go drinking with him, and in that way perhaps recover some of his money.

And what of us, the audience? What is our place in the final revel?

> SIMO. quin vocas
>   spectatores simul?
> PS.   hercle me isti hau solent
>   vocare, neque ergo ego istos;
>   verum sei voltis adplaudere atque adprobare hunc
>   gregem
>   et fabulam in crastinum vos vocabo.   (1331-34)

> SIMO. Why don't you invite the spectators along?
> PS. By heaven they don't usually invite me, so I won't invite them. Though if you want to applaud and acclaim this troupe, I'll invite you to another play tomorrow.

Our reward is that the playing shall go on, that comedy in perpetual renewal shall begin again tomorrow.

In his excellent article a few years ago, John Wright studied the metaphorical transformations of Pseudolus throughout the play as an analogy to the device of transformation and identification in Plautine language. He suggested that at the end of the play theatrical metaphors come to predominate, and indeed with the exit lines just read that Pseudolus is transformed into Plautus himself.

I would go further and place the emphasis rather differently. The key transformations of Pseudolus are more than linguistic, more than verbal metaphors. They are visual and improvisational. They are theatrical metaphors. In his control of the theatrical Pseudolus has, in a sense, been Plautus all through the play. Indeed the *Pseudolus* is a play about the Plautine process of play-making.

Plautine theatre is not mimetic in conception—it is metatheatrical. Plautus does not imitate life but a previous text. Whether that text came to him in written form or through the performances of South Italian theatre troupes, the narrative elements of most if not all of his play preexisted *as text*. Just so the narrative elements of the *Pseudolus* exist in the form of two letters (one from Calidorus' mistress, one from the *miles*) before the play begins. Pseudolus in the first scene resists and then decides to transform these plot elements through his own improvisatory energy and performance. This is the paradigm for Plautus' handling of a preexisting play.[30]

A tension between script and improvisation runs throughout the play, a tension often reflected in oppositions between mere words and theatre. Ballio commands where words are the issue, as in the *flagitatio* scene. His words can never rise to the level of theatre, however, try as he may in the final scene with Harpax. His "play" is merely a string of insults. Ballio's enemies, first the cook, then Pseudolus, can weave their words into theatre.

The identification of Plautus with Pseudolus naturally draws on Pseudolus' explicit and early self-identification with a poet: 404 *nunc ego poeta fiam.*[31] It is further enhanced by the scene between Pseudolus and Simia, a scene in which Pseudolus enacts the role of poet/creator. We noted earlier that traditional criticism has seen Pseudolus as curiously inactive in the play—but *we* can see that his major activity is in fact playwriting.[32]

An identification of Plautus with Pseudolus may also illumine

---

[30] We should note once again that it does not concern us whether one or two Greek plays went into the making of the *Pseudolus*. Two is perhaps more likely here. See Hough (1931).

[31] He is not quite unique in this. The parasite in *Asinaria* 748 is a poet as well, and Cleostrata is implicitly called a poet in *Casina* 861, for example.

[32] A footnote is the proper place for a little unbridled speculation on similarities between Plautine and Pseudolean style. There is an unusual emphasis on the triple in the *Pseudolus*, which I am at a loss fully to explain. Where in most Plautine comedies the emphasis is on the double, twins, and duplicity, in the *Pseudolus* our hero is usually in triple trouble (1024 *in metu sum maxumo triplici modo*) or plotting a triple cross (580 *triplicis dolos*; 691 *tris deludam*) or thrice crying beware (517). The great ephiphany of the triple is Pseudolus'

some curious features of the first scene between Pseudolus and Simia (905-55). There is a tinge of regret in the scene, a certain sadness hard to account for. Pseudolus certainly gets the worst of these exchanges. Why?

According to Leo,[33] Plautus came to Rome as an actor in the Atellan farce. Through its constant imitation of improvisation, Plautine theatre shows its creator's early training in this form: this is actor's, not director's, theatre. We also know from the didascalic notices that the *Pseudolus* was written in 191 B.C., and was therefore a late play; Cicero says that Plautus in his old age particularly enjoyed watching this play of his.[34]

Might we not read the Pseudolus/Simia scene as the old poet bidding farewell to acting?[35] Pseudolus begins as a consummate improvisatory actor. Simo greets him like an actor in their first scene when he comments on Pseudolus' acting style. Through acting the role of Surus, Pseudolus obtains the letter and the token that make the remainder of the play possible. For the completion of the play, though, Pseudolus can no longer act in his own play. He needs the services of Simia, who offers a strong challenge to Pseudolus' theatrical dominance. We have no positive statement from antiquity that Plautus was ever an actor, but there seems to be a deep personal regret expressed at the end of Pseudolus' dramatic career, which comes to an emphatic end in slapstick when Pseudolus falls offstage while dancing:

id fuit naenia ludo. (1278a)

That was the dirge for the game.

---

parody of tragedy: 703-5a *io te, te, turanne, te te ego, qui imperitas Pseudolo, / quaero quoi ter trina triplicia, tribu' modis tria gaudia, / artibus tribu' tris demeritas dem laetitias, de tribus / fraude partas per malitiam, per dolum et fallacias.* On one level the triple is appropriate to Pseudolus because he is one order more clever than any other *servus callidus*; on another, the triple itself is a feature of Plautine style. Plautus often expands by threes; see Fraenkel (1960), 341, n. 2, on the use of tricolon.

[33] Leo (1912), 63-86.

[34] Cicero, *de Senectute* 14.50.

[35] It could also be a general farewell to the stage, though certain features discussed below seem to me to tie it much more closely to acting.

Roman comedy, especially the slave parts Plautus wrote so well, was an acrobatic form of theatre. In his seventh decade Plautus would have been long past his performing prime. *Naenia* is a strong word, with its associations of death and mourning, but it is not particularly gloomy here. Perhaps the best translation one could offer for the phrase would be: "Our revels now are ended."

Indeed the analogy between the *Pseudolus* and Shakespeare's *Tempest* is striking. The *Tempest* is also a product of the latter stages of its author's career, and many have heard Shakespeare's voice in Prospero's when Porspero bids farewell to "the baseless fabric of this vision, the cloud-capp'd towers, the gorgeous palaces, the solemn temples, the great globe itself. . . ." Like Pseudolus, Prospero is also the masterful playwright of his own play, which must in the end dissolve.

In the end, though, such biographical inferences matter not at all. The meaning of the *Tempest* does not depend on whether Prospero is or is not Shakespeare bidding farewell to the Globe. Nor does the meaning of the *Pseudolus* depend on the identification of Pseudolus with Plautus himself. It depends rather on what the play says about theatre. Theatre celebrates itself in the *Pseudolus* as it does nowhere else in Roman comedy. Moreover, it celebrates through the character of Pseudolus himself and through his play-making the heady but anarchic mixture of script and improvisation, stock types and variations, illusory and non-illusory theatre that is Plautus' hallmark.

CHAPTER VIII

Convention and Reaction

Induction, frames, plays-within-plays, action half in and half out, on-stage audiences, disrupted plotting—at first sight the muddle is confusing. We may be looking for the wrong kind of unity, the unity of consistent action that belongs to modern realism. . . .[1]
—J. L. Styan

PLAUTUS' work offers us a study of the confluence of two traditions, that of Greek New Comedy and that of native Italian dramatic forms. Neither of those traditions, of course, has survived in substantial enough form for this statement to be explicitly provable, for no trace remains of preliterary Italian dramatic forms, and New Comedy, despite growing quantities of Menander, remains essentially "a strange country with a shadowy history."[2] Nor can this book attempt to consider in detail even the fragments of Menander that we do have. Nonetheless I believe we can go far in sorting out these two traditions solely through consideration of the use of non-illusory conventions and their functioning in the six texts we have studied here.

The two traditions can be broadly characterized by opposites. The native Italian forms were improvisatory, insofar as we can determine, like the much later popular Italian form of commedia dell' arte. By contrast, New Comedy had behind it two centuries of a tradition of scripted, literary drama. While improvisatory forms of dramatic expression doubtless existed in Greece, they were considered unworthy of the attention of literary historians in antiquity and seem by the fourth century to have exerted no recognizable influence on the high literary forms of tragedy and comedy.

The Atellan farce had a highly conventionalized set of roles or types, some of whose names are recorded.[3] No one could deny that

[1] Styan (1975), 218.
[2] Goldberg (1980), 13.
[3] See Duckworth (1952), 10-13. One might compare here something like

New Comedy was also characterized by conventionalized roles, as the existence of the stock masks in the performance tradition shows. We should not overemphasize this conventionalization in the time of Menander, however. While it is true that Menander himself uses a small and recognizable class of names for various types of characters,[4] we have no grounds for assuming that other writers of New Comedy did the same. Menander's names provide only a hint of character type and do not condition the action of the character. Role is not yet thought of as an entity that can exist independently of character. This is no small step: once the *servus currens* role or the *adulescens* role can be conceived of as distinct entities, the way for the comedy of role variation lies open.

Finally, the two traditions can be distinguished on the question of illusion. Greek New Comedy rejects the freedom of Old Comedy not only on political questions but also in artistic form. Aristophanes was free to shape his dramatic communication in many ways, some illusory, most not. New Comedy opts for the wall of illusion between audience and stage, for the indirect, representative means of dramatic communication that preserves a surface realism. Improvisatory comic forms always insist on retaining the option of direct stage/audience communication. To speak of illusion-breaking in these circumstances, then, is somewhat misleading. Since realism is merely another convention, we perhaps should rather speak of the non-illusory conventions and realism as alternatives. Plautus retains as many alternatives as he can.

As a first step toward synthesizing what is unique to Plautus' achievement within the medium of Roman comedy, let us look now

---

Ben Travers' Aldwych farces of the 1920's in Britain, where one role at least was sufficiently conventionalized to have its own designation: the "silly ass" part, of which an excellent example is D'Arcy Tuck in *Plunder*. People in the modern theatre may speak of an "ingenue" or the "juvenile lead," but these are descriptions of function and do not imply a standard characterization independent of the play in which they are contained.

[4] I think MacCary (1970) overstates his case when he argues that roles in Menander are fully conventionalized as those of the commedia dell' arte. Menander may have been experimenting with some such idea of typing characters by name, but if so it is his own idea, not a phenomenon of the whole theatrical world. MacCary makes his strongest case for Smikrines, less persuasive ones for Moschion and Chairestratos.

at his use and modification of the individual conventions. These have often in the past been abstracted and studied separately; we have used them above as windows into the meaning and workings of specific plays, emphasizing their function as devices for communication within the medium of performance. In our categorical review of Plautus' use of non-illusory conventions both in the six plays we have studied and in selected parallels from his other plays, the dimensions of his response to the two traditions he inherited should become clear.

Prologue and Epilogue

The usual view of the prologue in ancient drama has been that its function is informative. It exists primarily to give information about, or necessary to the understanding of, the play the audience is about to see—the ancient equivalent of the modern program with its indications of time and place or even a synopsis of the action. Plautus' prologues, by contrast, have as their primary goal not information but induction. Unlike Menander's omniscient divinities or Terence's artistic polemics, the prologue in Plautus seeks to draw the audience into the world of the play.

We must look beyond the two prologues we have dealt with in detail (that of the *Casina* indeed being mostly post-Plautine and therefore of no value in studying his technique) to other prologues in the corpus. These may be divided into three groups on the basis of character: divine prologues, prologues spoken by human characters within the play, and prologues delivered by uncharacterized or unidentified speakers.

Plautus does on occasion use divine prologue speakers, but only the Lar of the *Aulularia* prologue seems strictly equivalent to a Menandrean figure like Pan in the *Dyskolos*. The Lar speaks solely in character (which he reveals almost immediately, line 2), tells us the action about to ensue, and asserts his own role in causing the events (26 *feci*; 31 *faciam*). Arcturus in the *Rudens* is somewhat more prolix, and does step out of character to the extent of informing us indirectly that Diphilus is the author of the Greek original (32), but otherwise he does not differ from the Lar. Luxuria and Inopia, who serve as prologues to the *Trinummus*, move a little more in the direction of an <u>induction</u>. Luxuria refers to Plautus as her creator (8 *Plautus nomen Luxuriae indidit*) and gives us a translation history (18-21). In a motif we shall soon recognize as <u>typically Plautine</u>, she also <u>refuses to tell us anything about the plot, leaving that to the two old men who open the play</u> (16-17).

The divine prologue to the *Amphitruo* forms a transition to our next class of prologue, for Mercury, who speaks this fascinating and unsettling piece (1-152), is also a character within the drama about to be enacted. He begins with what must be one of the longest sentences in Plautus, a sixteen-line contract between player and audience: he will help them in their business dealings if they will give ear to the play. There is far more here than a bombastic parody of the Roman language of contract. This is a flatteringly phrased invitation into the world of the play that acknowledges the audience's part in creating that world. We might compare the Scrivener in Jonson's *Bartholomew Fair*, who makes a contract between playwright and audience in the induction of that play. A play is not a play unless someone watches it; the audience, Mercury acknowledges, are as important as the actors.

After some jokes about his father and master Jupiter, whom he will serve in this play disguised as the slave Sosia, Mercury proceeds to confuse and unsettle the audience's expectations of the play they are about to see. He first announces a tragedy, then pretends to change the nature of the play in the face of a negative reaction from the audience:

> post argumentum hujus eloquar tragoediae.
> quid? contraxistis frontem quia tragoediam
> dixi futuram hanc? deu' sum, commutavero.
> eandem hanc, si voltis, faciam ⟨jam⟩ ex tragoedia
> comoedia ut sit omnibus isdem vorsibus. (51-55)

Then I'll explain the plot of this tragedy. What? You're frowning because I said this was going to be a tragedy? I'm a god, I'll change it. If you wish, I'll make this same play into a comedy from a tragedy, with all the lines the same.

The audience reaction is perfectly predictable; as the prologue to the

Captivi says, it is not fair dealing with the audience to present a tragedy when they expect a comedy (61-62). However, Mercury's false alarm has the effect of unsettling genre expectations, a process reinforced when he introduces the term *tragicomoedia* (59-63).

Plautus concludes the inductive section of the *Amphitruo* prologue with a discussion of claques and warnings from Mercury that Jupiter forbids them. The first 96 lines have given us essentially no information about the play, but neither have they been a series of unrelated jokes. Plautus has rather used Mercury's jokes about the absurdity of the gods appearing in a comedy both to unsettle audience expectations, preparing them for the romantic and unusual plot of the *Amphitruo*, and to draw the audience into participation in the creation of the play, just as Mercury moves into his role as the slave Sosia.

The prologue to the *Mercator* is also spoken in character, here by the young lover Charinus, but Plautus has a comic point to make by use of a character, just as he does in the *Amphitruo*. Charinus specifically disavows the actions of other young lovers in comedies who tell their woes to the sun and the moon; he flatters and draws his audience in closer by addressing them directly (1-8).[5]

The third and most characteristic type of Plautine prologue has no name and as yet no assigned role. In his lack of specific character he parallels the state of the audience. Neither has as yet been drawn into the world of the play, where both player and audience will have their proper roles. These inductive prologues emphasize the theatricality of a play by making explicit the transition from one mode of perception to another, from the "realities" of the theatre to the imaginative space of the stage. The audience is thus drawn not into illusion but into participation in the creation and functioning of the play.

One purpose of such prologues may be puffery of the good qualities of the play about to begin. As we have already seen, the prologue of the *Asinaria* assures his audience that there are both *lepos* and *ludus* in the play we are about to see (13-14). The prologue of the *Captivi* assures his audience there are no dirty lines or hackneyed stock characters in the comedy he is about to present (56-62). Such

---

[5] In the opening scene of the *Curculio*, Plautus shows us how he could parody the same sort of scene in dialogue.

reassurances put the audience in a receptive frame of mind, as do the jokes and banter with members of the audience (cf. *Captivi* 11-14).

The next function of such a prologue is to create imaginative space. This may partly involve setting the scene, as the prologue of the *Menaechmi* does (69ff.), declaring this hitherto undefined space to be Epidamnus for the duration of the play (72 *dum haec agitur fabula*). The *Trinummus* prologue makes his stage into Athens, again for the duration of the play (10-11). The transition from reality to fiction, from actors to characters, may be explicitly acknowledged even as it takes place:

> haec res agetur nobis, vobis fabula. *Captivi* 52

> The action will be reality to us, a play to you.

The prologue to the *Poenulus* reminds us that he is leaving the stage to go put on his costume (123).

Finally, a striking feature of these inductive prologues is the repeated refusal to provide details of plot. We have already noted that the prologue of the *Trinummus* leaves the details to the old men who open the play (16-17). The *Asinaria*, as we have seen (8), assures us that the plot is no great problem. Even the fragmentary *Vidularia* 11 leaves the plot to be demonstrated through action.[6]

These uncharacterized prologues, then, have a far more important function than merely to provide information. They transform the audience's vision, create a playing space, and move both players and audience into their proper roles in the creation of the play. In this, Plautus' idea of the prologue stands in contrast to those both of his predecessor Menander and his successor Terence.[7]

---

[6] It is clear, then, that I disagree with Duckworth (1952), 211, when he says the primary purpose of the Plautine prologue was "to explain the *argumentum.*" His section on the prologue is a valuable compendium of traditional literary views of Plautine drama, discussed in terms of suspense. I hope I have shown that the prologues can be viewed in a much more positive light, as examples of considerable skill in drawing the audience into the play world. See also K. Abel (1955).

[7] It also seems to stand in contrast to the practices of other writers of the *palliata*. Cf. the fragments of prologues from Caecilius (71, p. 494; 126, p.

Plautus can make other types of scenes function as inductions into the play and the modes of dramatic perception appropriate to the play. Epidicus' first monologue performs the work of an induction in his play. Even though we have already had one scene played out on stage before Epidicus delivers his monologue, no movement into the world of the play has been initiated yet. The first scene of dialogue between the two slaves in the *Epidicus* functions as an expository prologue would but *not* as a bridge between modes of perception.[8] For this the sight of Epidicus working himself into his part, into his *persona*, serves nicely. The audience is reminded of the type of play this is to be: a work of role-playing with Epidicus in the starring role. As the audience experiences Epidicus' transition into his role, they undergo a similar transition into their own role and the sympathies that go with that role. No longer are they stolid Roman burghers, burdened by *pietas* and *gravitas*, but liberated Saturnalian revellers themselves. This escape from one role into another is a vital feature of the power and achievement of Plautine drama.

The induction scene in the *Bacchides* functions in much the same way. The lost prologue apparently was expository but not inductive.[9] Pistoclerus must be seduced into the world of the play by the Bacchides, seduced away from his Roman virtues into the theatrical freedom of the role of the *adulescens amans*. Just as he is seduced into imaginative consent to the play world and its standards and operations, so is the audience. They too leave their real world and become role-playing participants in the great game of the play.

Plautus often marks the transition out of the play world with an epilogue. Epilogues are far more abbreviated than prologues, but even so they are more than an appeal for applause (which is all that is left of the epilogue in Terence). The form is often moralizing even when the content is not. The abbreviated tag-line that closes

---

514; 134, p. 518) and Naevius (1, p. 74; 15, p. 78; 21, p. 80; 69-71, p. 98) in Warmington (1938). There is no securely identified fragment of an epilogue in any of the remains of the *palliata*.

[8] With a tradition stretching back to the two slaves in Aristophanes' *Knights*, we might note.

[9] Quite understandable if Gaiser (1970), 65-69, is correct is surmising that a monologue of Pistoclerus functioned as a delayed prologue.

the *Epidicus* (732-33) nonetheless finds room implicitly to praise *malitia*. The *Mercator* epilogue (1015ff.) offers a firm condemnation of old men who run after young girls, but there is also a sly appeal for applause aimed at the young men, who will benefit most if the proposed *lex* against the old is approved. The first three lines of the *Casina* epilogue are probably a post-Plautine addition, designed to fill out the story, but the remaining four (1015-19) promise that the revelry can continue after the play is over—if only the audience will applaud. The world of comic freedom need not be left behind. The *Cistellaria* epilogue (782ff.) emphasizes the transition out of the play world with its reference to the players remaining inside and removing their costumes. The *Bacchides* epilogue is more hesitant, and seems to feel a need to defend the play's existence (1207-11). We may only speculate that it dates from the time of one of those periodic moves toward "cleaning up the stage." Even so, the epilogue itself offers no explicit condemnation of what has gone on in the play. By repeating the seduction/induction scene from the beginning of the play with the old men as fresh objects at the end of the play, Plautus offers some hope of the renewal of the comic cycle.

The epilogue of the *Asinaria* offers the best hope of all (942-47). It promises us that, by our applause, we can save old Demaenetus from the beating he so richly deserves. By inviting belief in the continuing reality of the old man and his predicament, the epilogue paradoxically undercuts the realism of the play from an unexpected direction. The play has not been a representation or mimesis of reality but rather has an ongoing life even when not represented on the stage—yet only the theatre can play with such a notion. Only the joyously non-illusory theatre can play with the idea that a character has slipped off stage and out the back door and now lives his own life somewhere outside the theatre in which he had been trapped for the last hour or two.

The prologue and epilogue in Plautus, then, seem to function not as conventions designed to transmit as briefly as possible the information necessary to understand the play but rather as transitions between nontheatrical and theatrical modes of perception—and of course as opportunities for games-playing in and of themselves. The jokes and banter that seem so irrelevant to a reader actually perform a vital function in alerting the audience to its role in the play and in the workings of the theatre.

Monologue and Soliloquy

In all such scenes the aside and soliloquy are conventions inseparable from role-playing in non-illusory theatre: they persisted to the end of the nineteenth century when the naturalistic movement overtook the stage. These devices imply a complicity between actor and audience in the pleasure of putting on a play. The view that their apparent purpose was merely to inform the spectator of what was passing in a character's mind, like an interior monologue in the modern novel, is the mistake of superficial, anachronistic, and literary thinking.[10]
—J. L. Styan

A detailed comparative study of monologue technique in Menander and Plautus lies beyond the scope of the present work. In general, Plautus' reaction to Menander seems less pronounced here than elsewhere, simply because Menander admits the use of this non-illusory technique in his drama more often than any others.[11] A study of the theatrical functioning of the monologue in the ancient theatre, however, remains overdue, and so a few remarks on Plautus' use of the technique are in order.

A monologue may simply introduce a character and establish his type for the audience. We have seen above the elaborate induction Plautus makes of Epidicus' soliloquy near the beginning of his play. Perhaps the germ of such a move into character lies near the surface in any introductory monologue, for we see hints of it even in a simple entrance monologue like that of Mnesilochus in the *Bacchides* (385ff.). He enters moralizing on the nature of friendship. Not only does this serve what seems to have been a demand on the part of the Roman audience for such moralizing, it also helps establish his character. As he moves himself into the role of *adulescens amans* at the end of his soliloquy, his idealism and desire to be noble show forth:

> nunc, Mnesiloche, specimen specitur, nunc certamen
>   cernitur
> sisne necne ut esse oportet, malu', bonus quoivis modi,

[10] Styan (1975), 153.
[11] See most recently Blundell (1980). His formal classifications of monologues, though, tell little about their theatrical functioning. On Plautine monologue in general, see Fraenkel (1960), 135-201.

justus injustus, malignus largus, comincommodus.
cave sis te superare servom siris faciundo bene.
utut eris, moneo, hau celabis. (399-403)

Now, Mnesilochus, the truth will out, the contest will be
decided, whether or not you are what you ought to be, a
scoundrel or a good fellow—whatever—just, unjust, stingy,
generous, well or ill-mannered. Watch out that you don't let
your slave outdo you in good-deed-doing, if you please.
Whatever you're going to be, I'm telling you, there's no way
you'll hide it.

In much the same way, Philolaches' monologue in the *Mostellaria*
(84-156) introduces him to the audience and establishes his dreamy,
philosophizing character. Additionally, this speech serves to introduce a key image in this play, that of the house.[12]

After a character has been introduced, a soliloquy can be used
to establish or strengthen the speaker's hold on the audience's sympathies. After the scene in the *Casina* where the lot has fallen to
Lysidamus and Olympio, the audience's sympathies may be momentarily confused. After all, should not the *senex* be allowed his
little fling in the Saturnalian spirit of the day? Chalinus' ensuing
soliloquy (424-36) gives us the answer: no. His hurt and anger
arouse our sympathies: his despair is so great at first that he meditates
on suicide. Near the end of his soliloquy, though, he is presented
with a chance to eavesdrop on his victorious rivals and thereby gains
an opportunity for revenge. As his spirits rise, he carries our sympathies with him.

Somewhat similar is the monologue of Palaestra in the *Rudens*,
whom we have already heard of through the description of her
struggles in the surf. Now with her monologue (185-219) she establishes a firm hold on the audience's sympathies. The informational
content is minimal; the emotional tonality is the central message.

A monologue like that of Epidicus at 158ff. has no other
purpose than to involve the audience. The informational content
(that Epidicus intends to storm the old man: 163) is scarcely a

---

[12] See Leach (1969).

surprise. Nonetheless by portraying the moment of decision in Epidicus' monologue, Plautus once again engages the audience's sympathy through the direct confrontation of soliloquy.

The appeal of the soliloquy can even be through direct audience address. Gelasimus, the parasite in the *Stichus* (155-233), begins with what seems a normal soliloquy and ends by attempting to auction himself off to the audience. Plautus here provides us with an eavesdropper in the person of Crocotium to guide audience response through her asides. Here, as in most direct appeals to the audience (cf. old Lysidamus in the *Casina*), the effect is more to create humor than sympathy.

The soliloquy can be used to shock the audience into a new way of looking at a character. The preeminent example must be Toxilus' opening soliloquy in the *Persa*. It is short and its contents no more than a statement that the speaker is in love, without funds, and therefore unhappy. Yet it is enough profoundly to unsettle the audience's whole set of expectations based on stock character and type in the plays. By presenting this as a soliloquy, Plautus has challenged the audience as no simple prologue or report by another character of Toxilus' love affair could. The soliloquy confronts the audience directly, and the impact of Plautus' novel characterization of the slave is proportionately increased. Stratophanes' rejection of the role of *miles* in the *Truculentus* (482-98) is much more direct but no less effective for its humor.

Plautus attempts to reorient audience perception of character through Cleostrata's opening monologue in the *Casina* as well (148-64). The *matrona* in Roman comedy is usually a figure of repression—if not strictly an agelast, at least a reminder of the non-holiday world from which the sympathetic characters seek to escape. From the moment we see her mask, this is what we expect of Cleostrata. Plautus, though, wishes to portray the *matrona* here in a sympathetic light. By allowing her a soliloquy, Plautus lets her bring her case for sympathy directly to the audience.

Even more radical transformations of expectation through soliloquy are possible. Some will be discussed in the next chapter on metatheatre, such as Chrysalus' two key soliloquies in the *Bacchides*. In the first he declares his superiority to the usual stock part of clever slave; in the second he proclaims his unwillingness to remain in his own play. Here the confrontational aspect of monologue is pushed to its extreme, but the potential to confront and unsettle audience expectations is present in any such address.

Aside

The aside is fully as powerful a confrontation with the audience as the soliloquy, but with the added dimension of shaping our view of a scene of dialogue. The aside imposes a second layer of imaginative activity on top of the activity portrayed through dialogue. Asides are sometimes divided between those that occur within a scene of dialogue and those that seem to form a transition between scenes or between monologue and dialogue. This distinction does not seem theatrically meaningful, deriving as it does from the limited perspective of realism that finds the latter less offensive than the former, and will not be used here.

We can see, however, that an aside just before dialogue commences can shape our whole view of a scene. We can see this at work in as simple a scene as that in which Chrysalus in the *Bacchides* approaches Nicobulus. He announces that he intends to make the old man into the ram of Phrixus and shear him of golden fleece (239-42). Such a scene as the one Chrysalus is about to play with old Nicobulus may need no special interpretation, but the aside functions to whet the audience's anticipation of the scene. Moreover, the aside launches the sequence of sheep images which will be very important in this play; the immediacy of the aside is calculated to fix the poetic image more readily in the audience's mind.

The aside is often regarded as a convention designed as a means of revealing the inner thoughts of a character in a situation; in fact, this is merely the simplest and most obvious use of the aside. Plautus, like any other comic dramatist, is not above exploiting this type of aside for immediate effect, as for example in the *Casina*:

CL. enicas.
LY. vera dicas velim.
CL.   credo ego istuc tibi.   (233-34)

CL. You're killing me.

LY. I wish I were.
CL. *There* I believe you.

Even here Plautus plays with this homicidal aside by allowing Cleo-strata to overhear it and react to it. A little later Lysidamus shows the first signs of his penchant for the Freudian slip (365-68), as he tells his wife he wishes Casina to be given to himself—no, he means to his slave Olympio. The comedy here lies in the confusion over what he intends to say to his wife and what he should rather say aside. The audience enjoys the spectacle of a player who seems to have forgotten which way he should throw certain key lines.

The power of the aside should never be underestimated. When in the *Bacchides* Nicobulus bursts from his house in a rage over the deceptions that have been practiced on him, Chrysalus welcomes him with one brilliant punning aside:

salvos sum, iratus est senex. (772)

I'm safe, the old man is angry.

Through the pun on a famous proverb (see above, pp. 108-9), our whole view of the scene is transformed, and five simple words establish the theatrical superiority of Chrysalus in the scene that follows. The aside links player to audience through the ability to share a joke or a position of superior knowledge (most apparent in the eavesdropping scenes, for which see below). The player speaking the aside and the audience become allies in the fight against whatever enemy has currently taken the stage against them.

A surprising number of asides in Plautus deal with playing style. The *servi callidi* are always telling each other or themselves how to play a particular scene. When in the *Asinaria* Leonida is playing the part of the overseer Saurea—and in fact overplaying—Libanus slips in a quick aside to warn Leonida that in fact they are in danger of having their audience walk out on them: *heus jam satis tu* (446). Similarly, Milphidippa and Palaestrio congratulate each other in asides on their skill at playing the scene in *Miles Gloriosus* (1066) where they delude the *miles* with the tale of the matron who is madly in love with him. The audience is privileged to hear the actors discuss among themselves the fine-tuning of a performance. Given the camaraderie between players and audience implied by the very nature of the aside, the audience in this situation therefore has the feeling that it participates in the creation of the play. Toxilus in the *Persa* tells us directly how he intends to play the scene he is about to play with the parasite Saturio (84). A little later in the same play the would-be *servus callidus* Sagaristio tells us how he intends to play his upcoming scene with Toxilus, wherein he will in effect challenge Toxilus for control of the play (306-7 *graphice . . . gloriose*).

The aside is intimately associated with the idea of role-playing, because it is the obvious device for a performer to use when it is necessary for him to warn the audience that he has adopted a role. When Pardalisca bursts from the house in the *Casina* to announce that Casina has gone homicidally mad, she soon shares with the audience the kowledge that her hysterics are merely a role, adopted to frighten old Lysidamus (685-88). The aside can also interpret another's role as well as one's own. Periplectomenus in the *Miles* has an extended aside (200-18) in which he interprets the poses that the slave Palaestrio adopts—and thereby shows the audience how Palaestrio gradually works himself into the role of *servus callidus*, commenting on the playing style all the while (213 *dulice et comoedice*).

The aside, then, is a powerful and variegated device in Plautus. It effects a profound theatrical transformation of any scene wherein it is employed as it, momentarily or for a more extended period, gives us a double vision of the scene. Sometimes this double vision can be inside and out, the characters' thoughts opposed to their external behavior, but the aside in Plautus is by no means limited to this simple use. The aside can set source against parody, type against variation. Always it is a reminder of the special nature of communication in drama that allows us to receive two or more messages simultaneously.

Role-Playing

Plautine theatre, then, is a theatre of role-playing. The concept of role seems in Plautus to owe more to his Italian background than to the ethical spirit of Greek New Comedy. Many things are fathered upon the (fortunately for some scholars) no longer extant Atellan farce, but I believe we can see in its rigid conception of role and type the opportunity to do as Plautus did—to indulge in the comedy of role transferral. Much could be said about the adoption of role in general in Plautus. We have glanced at one obvious example: Leonida's adoption of the role of the slave-overseer Saurea in the *Asinaria*. We have seen Epidicus the *servus callidus* and Mnesilochus the *adulescens amans* as they put on the roles in their introductory monologues. We have also seen Pistoclerus in the *Bacchides* seduced into his role as *amator*. Calidorus in the *Pseudolus* enjoys his role as helpless *adulescens amans* so much that he is reluctant to give it up, and defends his playing of his role thus:

> non jucundumst nisi amans facit stulte.   (238)

There's no fun unless the lover plays the fool.

No doubt the audience agreed with him in general, but Pseudolus forces him to adopt whatever role Pseudolus wills. The *lena* of the *Asinaria* is not about to give up her usual role either. It is her duty and function to bleed the young lover for every penny he has, and she will not shirk her duty (173-75).

Roles that are so clearly defined can therefore be transferred among various characters and yet remain recognizable. The type behavior can be played against a mask that dictates a different type for effective comedy—comedy that is possible only in a theatre of role-playing. The obvious examples are the *senes* (old men) who forget their years and become *adulescentes amantes* (young lovers) again. To judge from Demaenetus in the *Asinaria*, Lysidamus in the *Casina*, and Nicobulus and Philoxenus in the *Bacchides*, the Roman audience never tired of the comedy of this particular role reversal. Cleostrata in the *Casina* effects the far more interesting (to us, at any rate) and heroic role transformation from *matrona* into the plot-manipulating poet role usually associated with the *servus callidus*. Role transferral can also be dangerous, though. When Lysidamus rejects the usual role of *senex amator* he ends up degraded to the position of a fugitive slave. Usually only one character in a play is strong enough to be master of the role transferrals, and in the *Casina* that character is not Lysidamus but Cleostrata.

The adoption of role is an obvious means for the comic trickster to attain his goals, and many scenes of role-playing show us either the *servus callidus* or an imitator using such means. We have seen Sagaristio in the *Persa* (543ff.) playing a "Persian" anxious to unload a slave on the unsuspecting slave-dealer, Leonida in the *Asinaria* (407ff.) playing the steward Saurea in order to bilk the ass-dealer, and we can add the parasite Curculio in the play of the same name (391ff.) pretending to be the servant of an absent *miles* in order to claim the girl the soldier has left behind. Phronesium in the *Truculentus* (449ff.) adopts the role of recently delivered mother to squeeze yet more money out of the *miles* whom she claims as the father of the suppositious infant.

Finally, roles may be assigned to a player by another, more powerful player. Old Apoecides in the *Epidicus* thinks he has adopted the role of foolish old man on his own when he and Epidicus go to get the flute-girl (420-21 *adsimulabam: quasi / stolidum, combardum me faciebam*), but in fact it is a role assigned to him by Epidicus. The *servi callidi* who coach others through their roles in various tricks are too numerous to require mention; we need only point to their apotheosis in the great Pseudolus, who creates and coaches Simia through his role (*Pseudolus* 905ff.).

Eavesdropping and Play-within-the-Play

The world-stage concept is the very essence of the play-within-the-play idea.[13]
—Robert Nelson

The usual view of the convention of eavesdropping in Roman comedy holds that it is an unfortunate necessity imposed on the poet on the order of the convention that all action must take place out of doors. Much ink has been wasted in deploring the lack of realism in various scenes of Plautus where information is acquired through eavesdropping on some confidential conversation that nonetheless takes place in the middle of the street. It should be clear, however, that though an eavesdropper may acquire useful information from

[13] Nelson (1958), 30.

the seclusion of his hiding place, he has a far more important the-atrical function in interpreting the scene he eavesdrops on to the audience. Any comments he makes aside interpret, either explicitly or implicitly, the scene that both he and the audience are observing. In that he is also an audience of the scene, he and the members of the audience share a bond that inclines them to accept whatever judgment he passes upon that scene.

Chalinus' eavesdropping scene in the *Casina* shows us this in-terpretative function at work (437-514). Traditional criticism would say that the sole purpose of the scene is to acquaint Chalinus with Lysidamus' plans for a wedding night with Casina so that Chalinus in turn can inform Cleostrata of these plans. Actually, Chalinus serves a far more important function in giving us the proper per-spective on Lysidamus and his lusts.[14] Chalinus' shocked asides (e.g., 457 *quid, "amplecti"?*) shape our response to Lysidamus' rampant and catholic sexual desire. Chalinus' aside that labels Lysidamus and Olympio "wild boars" (476) also presents a key image in as direct a way as possible. Lysidamus' desires are labelled animalistic—and the eavesdropping/aside form leads the audience readily to assent.

In much the same way Diniarchus' presence transforms the first appearance of Astaphium in the *Truculentus* (95ff.). He has just introduced himself in a lengthy monologue (1-94), which has de-tailed how he has been impoverished by love—or rather courtesans. Astaphium's entering soliloquy could simply be a humorous turn on the greed of courtesans—but the presence of Diniarchus, whom Astaphium and her mistress Phronesium have victimized, consid-erably darkens the tone and embitters the stock humor of the scene.

There can be more than one eavesdropper to a scene, but their dialogue remains as immediate a means of dramatic communication to the audience as a direct aside would be. Only the eavesdropping frame around Ballio's great entrance scene in the *Pseudolus* prevents him from stealing the show. Pseudolus and Calidorus are able by their discussion of his performance as a performance to reclaim the scene; we recall Calidorus' comment: *magnufice* (194) with its over-tones of criticism (see above, pp. 122-23).

[14] It is of course possible that Cleostrata already knows of Lysidamus' plans (see above, pp. 74-75 and n. 12). In this case, the usual view of the eaves-dropping scene would be totally at a loss to account for its occurrence here.

Plautus can also play variations on the usual eavesdropping scene and its power distribution. A prime example is when Mnesilochus eavesdrops on Lydus and Philoxenus in the *Bacchides*. Mnesilochus learns that his friend Pistoclerus is being accused by Lydus of keeping a mistress. Mnesilochus knows a bit more about the situation than do the two he overhears: he knows of the existence of the Samian Bacchis. He does not know, however, of the existence of her Athenian twin, with whom Pistoclerus has indeed taken up. Consequently, he misinterprets what he hears. His position in the scene, then, does imply a power, but one that he can only use negatively, when he undoes all the work of Chrysalus up to this point in the play. Mnesilochus' failure has more to do with his own character than with the structural nature of the eavesdropping scene; he simply does not have the personal resources to be a playwright.[15]

A successful playwright like Toxilus in the *Persa* can effect a more interesting change in the functioning of the eavesdropping scene. He deliberately allows himself to be overheard in the opening of the play by the parasite Saturio (83-84), creating a scene to trap the parasite's imagination. He has reversed the usual positions of power through his own control of the fictional process at this point.[16] Later in the same play he and the pimp Dordalus eavesdrop on the dialogue of the "Persian" and the "Persian girl" as they discuss their first sight of Athens. The usual double nature of the eavesdropping scene becomes triple in the hands of Toxilus. By the form of the scene Dordalus should occupy a more powerful position than either of the two objects of the eavesdropping scene, but in fact he is the least knowledgeable and least powerful person in the scene. Toxilus can mark this by turning aside from Dordalus to deliver a line like 547: *ut contemptim carnufex!* Toxilus can address the audience directly; Dordalus cannot; and from the audience comes the power.

The eavesdropping scene is a rudimentary form of the play-within-the-play. The eavesdroppers form the audience of the internal

---

[15] A somewhat fragmentary scene from the *Cistellaria* (305ff.) shows similarities to this scene. The *senex* eavesdrops on a *meretrix*, whom he mistakes for the girl his son is in love with. She, however, purposely deceives the old man.

[16] As we have noted before, Milphidippa in the *Miles* (991ff.) does essentially the same thing.

play. Though the form emphasizes the theatricality of the situation, the relative powerlessness of those within the play, and powerfulness of those who watch, not all such scenes imply a sense of metatheatre. Nonetheless such scenes point the way for theatrical games with the nature of dramatic communication and the question of illusion. How far Plautus advanced along that way will be discussed in the next chapter.

Improvisation

Improvisation is not solely a feature of non-illusory drama; indeed, it is not strictly part of any literary form of drama, though in performance even the most tightly scripted drama demands the improvisatory powers of the actors to give life to the work.[17] Improvisation lies at the heart of Plautine drama, however, knitting the various conventions together in the joyous process of playing the play. Though it would seem that improvisation should by nature be antithetical to any sort of control, in practice (and in Plautus) not every player or character can improvise freely. To allow every player the freedom to improvise is to invite chaos. One player must take the lead, give the hints and perhaps even assign the parts to the other players, in order to shape the dramatic action. In Plautus this player is usually the *servus callidus* or one of his imitators.

After the detailed exposition of the activities of the slave heroes undertaken above, this point may perhaps seem too obvious to require proof, but let us nonetheless consider one or two examples. When Epidicus tells Periphanes the tale of the returning army and the courtesans waiting at the gates for their lovers to return (196ff.), he improvises easily the conversations he supposedly overheard and indeed becomes so involved with the sheer delight of story-telling that he nearly derails his own purpose with a digression on women's

[17] I use the term *improvisation* somewhat differently from the way Styan uses it in *Drama, Stage and Audience*, to which I am greatly indebted in this work. I have argued that Plautus seeks to represent in his literary drama the improvisational spontaneity of preliterary drama, presumably the Atellan farce. To repeat what I said in the introduction, then, by improvisation in Plautus I mean the literary imitation of the characteristics of true improvisation, and I avoid some more accurate but less euphonious label for this phenomenon such as pseudo-improvisation.

fashions (224ff.). Later in the scene he is shown to be improvising barely fast enough to keep one step ahead of the over-eager *senex* Periphanes. The great Chrysalus improvises the whole tale of the pirate ship that prevented him and his young master from bringing home the money they were sent to Ephesus to get in the *Bacchides*. This sense of improvisation increases the immediacy of a scene. Chrysalus must leave the stage to acquaint his master with the tale he has just concocted (364); had everything been concerted in advance, the slip-ups that add excitement to the *Bacchides* would not have occurred.

Improvisation imparts an urgency to the comic experience parallel to the urgency of the holiday mood: we have one day to make merry, so let us make the most of it. Planning in advance only wastes precious time. At the heart of the high-speed improvisation that fills many of Plautus' plays is the impetuosity of the comic spirit.

When nothing is planned in advance, the action is new each time. Improvisation preserves the vitality of a highly conventionalized form. Even if, as we have seen above, Plautus plays numerous games with the conventions of both the Greek and Italian theatrical traditions as they were transmitted to him, it is the improvisational spirit that makes those games possible and always fresh and new.

Summary

The vitality of a convention is in its joyous capacity
for being inflected or subverted.[18]
—J. L. Styan

The broad outlines of Plautus' reaction to, and manipulation of, the conventions of Greek New Comedy should now be clear. Plautus reacts against Menandrean illusionism by emphasizing the theatricality of his plays. Where Menander sought to imitate life, Plautus seeks to have fun with the very idea of imitation. The prologue and epilogue frames mark the borders between reality and the world of the stage. The soliloquies confront the audience and demand that it take a stand, make a perceptual contribution to the process of play-making. The asides induce a theatrical double vision

---

[18] Styan (1975), 12.

that both produces an enjoyable irony and exemplifies the multi-dimensionality of the non-illusory theatre. Roles are taken up and dropped, transferred and subverted. Eavesdropping scenes turn into play-within-the-play, and all the while some improvising player struggles, not always successfully, to hold this unruly, boisterous, but vital enterprise to some narrative thread. This is far more than a burlesque of sentimental Greek comedy, as is often charged; it is a theatrical reconceptualization.

CHAPTER IX

Playwriting as Heroism

Plautus creates comedy by keeping both his audience and his characters safely aloof from the plot, from their own words, and from the very conventions on which his own plays depend.[1]
—John Wright

WE HAVE by now established the non-illusory nature of Plautine drama. Illusion was never the central goal of Plautus in his plays, as it seems to have been for Menander. Plautus admits the idea of illusion at times, but to look solely for illusion and complain when it is absent is totally to misunderstand the nature of Plautine theatre. If the preceding discussions have better elucidated the way Plautus' plays functioned in the theatre for which they were written and shown how the remarkable celebratory release and Saturnalian revel in these plays was a specifically theatrical experience achievable only in the theatre, then the great part of my purpose will have been accomplished.

It remains, however, to consider the phenomenon of metatheatre in Plautus. As I cautioned in the introduction, not all non-illusory drama is in fact metatheatre. It might be argued that all the non-illusory conventions discussed in the last chapter are the common property of comedy, that all comic theatre plays games with itself and with the idea of illusion. Comedy is a reactive form, and constantly plays variations not only on "serious" drama (e.g., through parody of tragedy) but also on itself. What special claim for a different kind of theatrical consciousness can be made for Plautus?

In answering this question we must first recall the unique position of a dramatist like Plautus. A working professional in the native Italian dramatic forms, he set himself the task of turning the plays of an alien tradition of theatre, Greek New Comedy, into playable Latin versions, a process he describes as *vortere*. It is rel-

---

[1] Wright (1974), 148.

atively rare, at least in our day, for a practical man of the theatre to be properly equipped to do such translating and adapting. More often the work falls to a man of letters with an interest in the theatre but without any practical backstage experience of it.[2] Such a belles-lettreist was Terence. His plays show the marks of his lack of practical theatre experience. He evidently thought little of the native Italian traditions, and used elements of them only grudgingly in his plays.

As a working man of the theatre, Plautus cannot but have been aware of the sharp differences between the Italian drama he knew and the Greek drama he was adapting. The Plautine process of composition is the very paradigm of metatheatre: he imitates not life but a previous text. Plautine theatre, then, is not mimetic in nature but metatheatric.[3]

Consequently, theatre and playing style are constant subjects of Plautine drama. The play continually comments on itself and how it is being played. The prologues naturally discuss the play that is to follow, but in ways that call attention to the theatricality of the enterprise. Monologues confront the audience with the idea of character in the theatre and can stand the usual ideas of character on ear. Highly conventionalized forms of theatre rely on adherence to a strict set of rules in order to communicate with the audience. Plautus simply scrambles the rules at times—and always calls attention to

[2] It cannot have been all that common, even in the often bilingual Mediterranean culture of Plautus' day, for a man of the theatre to have had sufficient command of literary Greek to adapt plays. This ability to translate plays remains relatively rare today, which may account for the fact that there are, for example, so few playable Ibsen translations. One striking exception is the playwright Tom Stoppard, who has a considerable reputation for his own work and yet translates and adapts the work of others for the English stage as well. It is well worth noting that he, like Plautus, is also fascinated with the very idea of theatre and the nature of illusion in the theatre. I do not mean to imply that there is any shortage of academic translations of plays, whether ancient or modern. The number of these that will hold the stage, however, is a small proportion indeed.

[3] Clearly there is a development in this direction in Plautus' work. The plays considered here were chosen for the metatheatrical features they display, and most seem to fall nearer the end than the beginning of Plautus' career. Plautine chronology, except for the two dated plays, is so disputed that I would not wish to place too much weight on this argument.

the theatrical process thereby. Asides constantly comment on playing style. These asides usually come from the *servi callidi*. Most *servi callidi* comment only on how they will play (or are playing) their own scenes, but Chrysalus in the *Bacchides* not only feels free to criticize Pistoclerus' acting style, he manages to slip in an advertisement for Plautus' *Epidicus* as well (214). The role-playing and the improvisation also constantly call attention to the play as play.

Metatheatre is more than simply the use of the device of the play-within-the-play. If we return to Abel's summation of metatheatre in the two propositions that "the world's a stage" and "life is a dream," we have at least established the first for Plautus' theatre. If Plautine drama represents any world, that world is the stage itself. Its characters are of players and playwrights, its plots the most theatrical of plots, its settings theatrical settings.[4]

But is life a dream? And if so, what sort of a dream is it? Who dreams the dream? Aside from two plays structured around unwitting doubles in which waking and dreaming is thematically important (the *Amphitruo* and the *Menaechmi*), the "life is a dream" analogy seems not to have greatly preoccupied Plautus. Two actual dreams that foreshadow the action of the play are reported by characters (in *Mercator* 225ff. by Demipho, and *Rudens* 593ff. by Daemones). There is, however, no continuation of the conceit throughout either play, nothing to suggest a dreamlike quality to experience.

What little evidence there is suggests rather that the plays contain two classes, those who dream and those who wake. The romantic and ignorant are those who dream, like Phaedromus, the young hero of the *Curculio*, who claims to be asleep and dreaming when he embraces his sweetheart:

> PA. . . . quin tu is dormitum?
> PH.   dormio, ne occlamites.
> PA. tuquidem vigilas.
> PH.   at meo more dormio: hic somnust
>   mihi.
>
> (183-84)

---

[4] As an example of the last, we might consider Simia's question of Ballio at line 971 of the *Pseudolus: ecquem in angiporto hoc hominem tu novisti?* As the *angiportum* is a stage street, we are reminded once again that this world is the stage.

PA. Why don't you go to bed?
PH. I *am* sleeping, don't shout so.
PA. In fact you're wide awake.
PH. No, I'm sleeping after my own fashion; this is my dream.

In both the *Menaechmi* and the *Amphitruo*, references to sleep and dreams abound. In the *Amphitruo* the language of sleep and dreams is consistently used of and by the human characters, while in the *Menaechmi* such references most often concern the visiting Syracusan twin.[5] As one example, we might consider Amphitruo's proffered explanation of the account Sosia has just given him, and Sosia's emphatic denial:

AM. ibi forte istum si vidisses quendam in somnis Sosiam.
SO. non soleo ego somniculose eri imperia persequi.
    vigilans vidi, vigilans nunc ⟨ut⟩ video, vigilans
        fabulor,
    vigilantem ille me jam dudum vigilans pugnis
        contudit.

(621-24)

AM. Perhaps that was some Sosia you saw in your dreams there.
SO. I don't usually carry out my master's orders by sleep-walking. I saw it wide awake, as now I'm seeing wide awake, and I'm wide awake telling the story. That fellow was wide awake just now when he punched my wide-awake face.

It is clear in the *Amphitruo* at least that the play is a dream, sent by the gods (here physically present in the play) to mortals. Both *senes* who tell their dreams in *Mercator* and *Rudens* say in identical couplets (*Mercator* 225-26 = *Rudens* 593-94) that the gods send dreams like plays to men; in the *Amphitruo* they send a play like a dream.

[5] See Segal (1969), 77-93. Segal proposes that the whole play is the dream of Menaechmus of Epidamnus, who has conjured up a surrogate self in the person of his twin.

Other evidence suggests that those who wake in a play have at least a godlike vantage-point, if not godlike powers over the sleepers as well. Tranio in the *Mostellaria* in an aside to the audience comments that the old men he has duped are "asleep" (829 *specta, quam arte dormiunt*). We the audience and Tranio, then, are by implication awake; we are superior to the unfortunate *senes* wrapt in the dream Tranio has spun for them.

Life is a dream only for some in the world of Plautus. The young lovers and the deluded old men dream their lives away, but the comic tricksters are fully awake. It may indeed be necessary to rouse the *architectus doli* to adopt his proper character, as Periplectomenus does Palaestrio in the *Miles* (215 *vigila, ne somno stude*). Once awake, the tricksters manipulate those who dream, but are not caught up in dreams themselves.[6]

Plautine metatheatre is thus quite different from that described by Abel in the Renaissance and after. Life is not seen as equally theatricalized for all. The stage world divides into players and playwrights, poets and poetic material.[7]

To be sure, the playwright's success is not guaranteed in such a world. The string of poetic failures in the *Asinaria* stands as warning: only a singularly powerful character can dominate and direct an entire play. The achievement of such a poetic self is the first step in that direction; in the case of Epidicus, such a self is the chief project of his play.

The other plays demonstrate how far the force of a powerful, organizing player can go in shaping the rest of the players and the play to his will. Let us look again, then, at four of the plays and see what vision of the stage and the leading player they project through metatheatre.

---

[6] Except by their own choice, e.g., Toxilus in the *Persa*.

[7] Abel would seem to imply that heroism is not possible in metatheatre. In general he emphasizes the "speculative sadness" (Abel [1963], 59) of the plays' endings, and in his summary of the differences between metatheatre and tragedy (p. 113) does not even allude to possibilities for heroism in either form. He admits the possibility that a character can create a new and happy ending for a play with tragic possibilities (see his discussion of *Life is a Dream* and Basilio's successful ending to his play, 71-72), but he seems to regard this as exceptional and not heroic. I shall argue that in Plautus, at least, such metatheatrical heroism is the norm; any sadness, such as that hinted in the ending of the *Pseudolus*, is for human limitation as opposed to theatrical possibility.

THE *PERSA* must be one of Plautus' most unabashedly joyous theatre games. It takes the standard New Comedy plot and tears it free from its usual upper-class setting, restaging the play at the bottom rungs of the social ladder, among the slaves, pimps, and parasites. The restricted world of the well-to-do burghers of the Hellenistic cities is swept aside.

In this world the clever slave Toxilus reigns supreme. With his master and his master's free society exiled from the stage for a day, he is free to do what no other *servus callidus* in Plautus does: intrigue on his own behalf. Toxilus has fallen in love. Not only is this a fundamental change in the nature of the slave character, it is clearly an aggrandizement of the role. The slave suddenly has an emotional life, a remarkable innovation in an ancient society, given the usual view of the slave as not quite human. Even though this side of Toxilus' character is not developed in any detail, he has moved to enlarge the range and possibilities of his part.

In the process he has also retained all the elements of the *servus callidus* part, as he establishes in his confrontation with Sagaristio. Sagaristio could conceivably move into the *servus callidus* part, and makes a serious bid to do so by providing money at a key moment in the intrigue. Toxilus easily deals with this challenge and demonstrates that with the plan he has conceived he could achieve his goal even without Sagaristio's help. That help only allows a slight reordering of the deception for ease of execution.

Toxilus creates the action of the latter part of the play with the false letter from his master that he writes. He in effect writes the play through the letter. Through it he manipulates Dordalus as a character (he gives him a speech thereby) and achieves his personal dramatic success.

The komastic ejnding of the *Persa* is far from an afterpiece, as has sometimes been suggested. It is rather a celebration of the extended theatrical dimensions of the character of Toxilus. Toxilus has achieved not only a personal victory in winning Lemniselenis for himself but also a dramatic victory in making a fool of the pimp. His dramatic victory is given an encore performance during the concluding *komos* as Paegnium, under orders from Toxilus (843 *graphice hunc volo ludificari*), abuses Dordalus. Toxilus then has succeeded in making a play out of Dordalus—and by implication has reified himself. The *Persa* is a study in theatrical self-creation.

Once again we must be aware of the danger of metaphor. How can a character actually be theatrically self-creating? I may seem to conflate the activities of Plautus and the activities of his hero here. In fact, Plautus takes care to demonstrate that Toxilus controls the play. Chance plays no fundamental part in the working out of the action. All of the action flows from the character of Toxilus, from his imagination and desires. He assigns the parts in the play and keeps the other players in line. Even when he allows Sagaristio and the "Persian" girl to improvise a scene for Dordalus' benefit, it is under his watchful eye. He even risks the loss of his immediate goal by insisting that Dordalus interview the "Persian" girl himself, because he is unwilling to allow part of his play to be unplayed. He could not love Lemniselenis so much, loved he not theatre more.

CHRYSALUS in the *Bacchides* is also theatrically self-creating, in ways that delineate his reaction against the confines of his stock role. He arrives when the play is already underway, and effects a solution to young Mnesilochus' problems with one elaborate, improvised deception speech to the old man. His use of the traditional tools of deception comes undone through Mnesilochus' ignorance, and Chrysalus then must solve the problem of the play a second time, in this instance through a more literary form of dramatic creation. Through his letters he writes the rest of the play.

Like Toxilus, Chrysalus is a literary playwright. He dictates the course of the play through the letter he dictates to Mnesilochus. More clearly than in any other play, the action of the *Bacchides* is the literary creation of the clever slave. Unfortunately (from his point of view) Chrysalus has not succeeded in writing a new role for himself in the process.

Even before he learns of the failure of his first scheme, Chrysalus is dissatisfied with his role as given to him. In a soliloquy he proclaims his own superiority to the usual comic slaves who cheat their masters (649-50). Even if the original audience did not know that he was thereby rejecting the *persona* he had had in his Greek incarnation, it would have been clear to them that Chrysalus was putting a distance between himself and his stock part.

After the success of his second scheme, he remains an unsatisfied player. He refuses to follow even the usual pattern of the *servus gloriosus* role. He refuses to play triumphing general for the audience (1072-73), a burlesque Roman audiences apparently found much to their taste; for Chrysalus it will not do, however, because it has become too common. As he would not be a common Greek slave, so he will not be a common Roman *servus gloriosus*.

Like Mnesilochus, Chrysalus finds only a negative solution to his dissatisfaction at the end of the play. Mnesilochus, believing himself deceived by his best friend, threw away the first play Chrysalus had created for him, even though he could not himself create another. Chrysalus, dissatisfied with the slave role he has been given, simply walks out of his own play at the end. Unlike Toxilus he has not yet discovered how to rewrite the role to his own satisfaction. Nonetheless his success as playwright in shaping other parts of the play points the way to the future.

CLEOSTRATA in the *Casina* is perfectly content with her role as *matrona*—so long as she can be playwright of her play as well. Her role as playwright of her own play is perhaps more explicitly delineated than that of any other character in the six plays, but she does not set out to be a playwright. Only because she cannot bear her husband's infidelities is she finally driven to take control of her own fate and that of the play.

Cleostrata is an unlikely playwright. Women, especially free women of good position, are not supposed to be active participants in the shaping of their own fates. Plautus introduces us gently to the idea of the *matrona* as playwright. After her hurt and angry soliloquy over Lysidamus' plans for Casina (531-38), she has a scene with Alcesimus in which she does—nothing. Yet nothing in this circumstance is an astonishing thing for her to do. She undoes Lysidamus' plan to get the wife of Alcesimus out of the way simply by refusing to respond to Alcesimus' hints in the scene. Alcesimus departs thoroughly baffled and frustrated. Cleostrata then rejoices in a short soliloquy that makes explicit her playwriting plans (558-62 *lepide ludificatus . . . ludificem . . .*). She starts her playwriting career in a small—one might even say negative—way, but she nonetheless begins.

By the time the ladies come out on stage to watch the play they have written unfold, the role of Cleostrata as playwright is perfectly clear. She has recruited Chalinus for the role of Casina and concocted the story of her madness. Cleostrata is exclusively a playwright at this point. She even leaves the final instructions to Pardalisca to deliver as mock advice to the bride. Cleostrata has only to sit back and wait until she reclaims her erring husband at the end.

Despite her playwriting activity, Cleostrata is the same character at the end of the play as at the beginning. Perhaps this is why her playwriting activity must be so clearly marked; she does not transform herself. Whatever the reason, she is content to use her playwriting powers solely to bend others to her will.

THE TITLE character of the *Pseudolus* is both playwright and player, both poet and performer. He too is restive in his role at first. He shows no sympathy for Calidorus' woes when the letter from Calidorus' mistress is first read. With his jokes he makes a game of the young man's distress, but eventually, whether he will or no, his mask draws him into the fray (see above on 107 *ita supercilium salit*).

When the "poet" soliloquy follows, we know Pseudolus' ambition: he no longer wishes to remain just a player, his role dictated by his mask. He will attempt to seize control of his own play. The arrival of Harpax offers him the opportunity, but in order to take advantage of it he must give one final, farewell performance as a player: he must enact the role of Surus, Ballio's overseer. This done and the letter and the token obtained, Pseudolus can retire from acting and devote himself instead to writing the rest of the play.

Pseudolus accomplishes this through the medium of Simia. Simia, for all his youthful theatrical energy (and the threat he temporarily poses to Pseudolus himself through his own powers of improvisation), remains finally only an actor. Simia neither wants nor receives a reward. Pseudolus introduces him into the play, uses him, and discards him.

Pseudolus the playwright remains to celebrate his dramatic victory. He enjoys the rewards of wine and women, and if there is regret for his acting career past there is also joy in his present powers as playwright. Though his self-creation is perhaps no longer limitless in that he has had to give up the *servus callidus* role, he nonetheless

176

has created a new role for himself that he fills quite comfortably: playwright and hero.

The clever slaves are the real heroes of these plays: their abilities make the plays possible. Indeed their playwriting abilities (whether literary or improvisatory) are the source of their heroism, a heroism that is more in the spirit of Aristophanes and Old Comedy than anything we find in New Comedy.[8] Not quite so limitless in their field of action as the heroes of Old Comedy, Plautine slave heroes still possess the imagination to remake their world and themselves.

Metatheatre in Plautus is the celebration of the power of the imagination. In this way Plautine drama differs rather sharply from many later metaplays. Life for the slaves is not a dream in Plautus: life is the harsh world of whips and crosses and nasty little wars among the epigonoi. Theatre is a dream. On stage, life can be reshaped by the imagination. Plautus' metatheatre is a new entity on the ancient stage. Unlike the fantasy world of Aristophanes which has the world for a stage, the dream in Plautus is explicitly theatrical: the transformation of reality happens only in the theatre and through theatrical means. The stage is his world.

Plautus was phenomenally popular in his own time. Had he had any successors who were as theatrically aware and imaginative as he, the course of Roman comedy might today comprise more than two surviving playwrights.[9] He did not, however. His obvious comic appeal kept his works alive even after their metatheatrical nature was no longer understood, as the later history of the *Pseudolus* shows. It remained for Calderon and Lope de Vega in the Spanish Golden Age to begin to experiment with metatheatre again.

Even though he had no immediate successors, Plautus' imag-

---

[8] This is not to say, of course, that Plautus had read Aristophanes or even knew his name (although see Chapter III, n. 20, for one suggested link). Konstan (1983), 164, finds Phronesium in the *Truculentus* Aristophanic in her refashioning of her world in the image of her own desires. His suggestion that this is to be linked to the "satiric" nature of that play misses the point. It is rather that an Aristophanic sense of the vast potential for recreating both the self and the world lies at the heart of comedy and could be rediscovered and revived by Plautus independently.

[9] The Roman comic impulse, and with it the playful penchant for subverting its own literary form, seems to have migrated to the Roman novel.

inative achievement in these plays remains for us to admire. He occupied a unique position at the confluence of two theatrical traditions and made the most of their creative collision. His plays enthralled the audiences of his day, influenced the shape of comedy in the Renaissance and after in more ways than we can recount, and remain today as a fascinating study in the power and range of the imagination.

I am sure that in the Roman Empire I was the leader of a troupe of strolling players, one of those who went to Sicily to buy women to make actresses of them, and who were at once professor, pimp, and performer. They are great characters, those rogues in Plautus' plays, and when I read about them they seem to evoke memories in me. Have you occasionally experienced something like that—the shiver of history?

—Flaubert in a letter to Louise Colet

The following does not pretend to be a comprehensive bibliography of Plautus. Its primary purpose is to give the full citations for those works cited in the footnotes. I have therefore not subdivided it according to play or topic. To those wishing to pursue a single play or issue, I commend the excellent bibliographies of Hanson (1965-66), Hughes (1975), and Segal (1981). Other bibliography can be found in Arnott (1979) and Goldberg (1981). As with most advances in dramatic criticism in the English language, Shakespearean studies have led the way in performance criticism, and so several works are cited here as important examples of methodology.

Abel, Karlhans. 1955. *Die Plautusprologe*. Mülheim-Ruhr.
Abel, Lionel. 1963. *Metatheatre*. New York.
Arnott, W. G. 1975. *Menander, Plautus, and Terence*. Oxford.
Bader, B. 1970. "Der verlorene Anfang der Plautinischen 'Bacchides.' " *Rheinisches Museum* 113: 304-23.
Bain, David. 1977. *Actors and Audience*. Oxford.
Barber, C. L. 1959. *Shakespeare's Festive Comedy*. Princeton.
Barchiesi, Marino. 1970. "Plauto e il 'metateatro' antico." *Il Verri* 31: 113-30.
Beare, W. 1963. *The Roman Stage*. 3rd. ed. New York.
Beckerman, Bernard. 1979. *Dynamics of Drama*. New York.
Bertini, F. 1968. *Plauti Asinaria*. Genoa.
Blundell, John. 1980. *Menander and the Monologue*. Göttingen.
Brook, Peter. 1968. *The Empty Space*. London.
Chiarini, G. 1978. "Casina o della metamorfosi." *Latomus* 37: 105-20.
Clark, John R. 1976. "Structure and Symmetry in the *Bacchides* of Plautus." *Transactions of the American Philological Association* 106: 85-96.
della Corte, F. 1951. "La commedia dell' Asinario." *Rivista di Filologia e di Istruzione Classica* 79: 298-306.
———. 1975. "Maschere e personaggi in Plauto." *Dioniso* 46: 163-93.
Dingel, J. 1978. "Menandrische Elemente im Epidicus des Plautus." *Philologus* 122: 14-24.
Duckworth, George E. 1940. *T. Macci Plauti Epidicus*. Princeton.
———. 1952. *The Nature of Roman Comedy*. Princeton.
Dumont, J.-Chr. 1977. "Le Persa, d'Aristophonte à Plaute?" *Revue de Philologie* 51: 249-60.
Elam, Keir. 1980. *The Semiotics of Theatre and Drama*. London and New York.
Ernout, Alfred. 1935. *Plaute: Bacchides*. Paris.
Forehand, Walter E. 1973. "Plautus' *Casina*: An Explication." *Arethusa* 6: 233-56.
Fraenkel, Eduard. 1960. *Elementi Plautini in Plauto*. Florence.

Frank, Tenney. 1933. "On the Dates of Plautus' *Casina* and its Revival." *American Journal of Philology* 54: 368-72.

Gaiser, Konrad. 1970. "Die plautinischen 'Bacchides' und Menanders 'Dis Exapaton.' " *Philologus* 114: 54-87.

Garton, Charles. 1972. *Personal Aspects of the Roman Theatre*. Toronto.

Gentili, Bruno. 1979. *Theatrical Performances in the Ancient World: Hellenistic and Early Roman Theatre*. Amsterdam.

Goldberg, Sander M. 1978. "Plautus' *Epidicus* and the Case of the Missing Original." *Transactions of the American Philological Association* 108: 81-91.

———. 1980. *The Making of Menander's Comedy*. Berkeley.

———. 1981. "Scholarship on Terence and the Fragments of Roman Comedy: 1959-1980." *Classical World* 75: 77-115.

Goldman, Michael. 1972. *Shakespeare and the Energies of Drama*. Princeton.

Gratwick, A. S. 1982. "Drama," in *Cambridge History of Classical Literature*, vol. 2: *Latin Literature*, ed. E. J. Kenney, pp. 77-138. Cambridge.

Greenblatt, Stephen. 1980. *Renaissance Self-Fashioning: From More to Shakespeare*. Chicago.

Guilbert, D. 1962. "La *Persa* de Plaute: une parodie de comédie bourgeoise." *Publications de l'Université de l'Etat à Elisabethville* 3: 3-17.

Handley, E. W. 1968. *Menander and Plautus: A Study in Comparison*. London.

———. 1975. "Plautus and his Public: Some Thoughts on New Comedy in Latin." *Dioniso* 46: 117-32.

Hanson, John Arthur. 1965. "The Glorious Military," in *Roman Drama*, ed. T. A. Dorey and Donald R. Dudley. New York.

———. 1965-66. "Scholarship on Plautus since 1950." *Classical World* 59: 103-9, 126-29, 141-48.

Hough, John N. 1931. *The Composition of the Pseudolus of Plautus*. Lancaster, Pa.

———. 1935. "The Development of Plautus' Art." *Classical Philology* 30: 43ff.

———. 1937. "The Structure of the *Asinaria*." *American Journal of Philology* 58: 19-37.

Hughes, J. David. 1975. *A Bibliography of Scholarship on Plautus*. Amsterdam.

Jocelyn, H. D. 1969. "Chrysalus and the Fall of Troy." *Harvard Studies in Classical Philology* 73: 135-52.

Katsouris, A. G. 1977. "Plautus' Epidicus = Menander's Homopatrioi?" *Latomus* 36: 316-24.

Kerr, Walter. 1967. *Tragedy and Comedy*. New York.

Knapp, Charles. 1919. "References in Plautus and Terence to Plays, Players, and Playwrights." *Classical Philology* 14: 35-55.

Knox, B.M.W. 1972. "Euripides' *Iphigenaia in Aulide* 1-163 (in that order)." *Yale Classical Studies* 22: 239-61.

Konstan, David. 1978. "Plot and Theme in Plautus' *Asinaria*." *Classical Journal* 73: 215-21.

———. 1983. *Roman Comedy*. Ithaca and London.

Lacey, Douglas N. 1978-79. "Like Father, Like Son: Comic Themes in Plautus' *Bacchides.*" *Classical Journal* 74: 132-35.

Leach, E. W. 1969. "De exemplo meo ipse aedificatio: An Organizing Idea in the *Mostellaria.*" *Hermes* 97: 318-32.

Leo, Friederich. 1912. *Plautinische Forschungen.* 2nd. ed. Berlin.

Little, Alan McN. G. 1938. "Plautus and Popular Drama." *Harvard Studies in Classical Philology* 49: 205-28.

MacCary, W. T. 1968. *"Servus Gloriosus*: A Study of Military Imagery in Plautus." [Ph.D. diss.] Stanford.

———. 1970. "Menander's Characters: Their Names, Roles, and Masks." *Transactions of the American Philological Association* 101: 277-90.

———. 1974. "Patterns of Myth, Ritual, and Comedy in Plautus' *Casina.*" *Texas Studies in Language and Literature* 15: 881-89.

———. 1975. "The Bacchae in Plautus' *Casina.*" *Hermes* 103: 459-63.

MacCary, W. T. and Willcock, M. M. 1976. *Plautus: Casina.* Cambridge.

Monaco, Guisto. 1964. "L'epistola nel teatro antico." *Dioniso* 38: 334-51.

Müller, Gerhard Ludwig. 1957. *Das Original des Plautinischen Persa.* Frankfurt.

Nelson, Robert J. 1958. *Play within a Play.* New Haven.

Nixon, Paul. 1916-1938. *Plautus.* 5 vols. Cambridge, Mass.

Pasquali, Giorgio. 1952. *Storia della tradizione e critica del testo.* 2nd. ed. Florence.

Petrone, Gianna. 1977. *Morale e antimorale nelle commedie di Plauto.* Palermo.

Pöschl, Viktor. 1973. *Die neuen Menanderpapyri und die Originalität des Plautus.* Heidelberg.

Questa, Cesare. 1970. "Alcune strutture sceniche di Plauto e Menandro." *Entretiens Hardt* XVI, pp. 181-215. Genoa.

Salingar, Leo. 1974. *Shakespeare and the Traditions of Comedy.* Cambridge.

Segal, Erich. 1968. *Roman Laughter.* Cambridge, Mass.

———. 1969. "The *Menaechmi*: Roman Comedy of Errors." *Yale Classical Studies* 21: 77-93.

———. 1981. "Scholarship on Plautus 1965-1976." *Classical World* 74: 353-433.

Sifakis, Gregory M. 1971. *Parabasis and Animal Choruses.* London.

Skutsch, Otto. 1914. "Ein Prolog des Diphilos und eine Komödie des Plautus." *Kleine Schriften* (Berlin): 184-96 (=*Rheinisches Museum* 55 [1900]: 272-85).

Sontag, Susan. 1966. *Against Interpretation.* New York.

Steegmuller, Francis. 1980. *The Letters of Gustave Flaubert 1830-1854.* Cambridge, Mass.

Styan, J. L. 1975. *Drama, Stage and Audience.* Cambridge.

Taplin, Oliver. 1978. *Greek Tragedy in Action.* Berkeley.

Tatum, James. 1983. *Plautus: The Darker Comedies.* Baltimore and London.

Theroux, Paul. 1975. *The Great Railway Bazaar.* New York.

Thierfelder, A. 1939. "Plautus und Römische Tragödie." *Hermes* 74: 155-66.

Torrance, Robert M. 1978. *The Comic Hero*. Cambridge, Mass.

Warmington, E. H. 1935-40. *Remains of Old Latin*. 4 vols. Cambridge, Mass.

Webster, T.B.L. 1970. *Studies in Later Greek Comedy*. 2nd. ed. New York.

Wheeler, A. L. 1917. "The Plot of the *Epidicus*." *American Journal of Philology* 38: 237-64.

Williams, Gordon. 1956. "Some Problems in the Construction of Plautus' *Pseudolus*." *Hermes* 84: 424-55.

Wright, John. 1974. *Dancing in Chains: The Stylistic Unity of the Comoedia Palliata*. Rome.

————. 1975. "The Transformations of Pseudolus." *Transactions of the American Philological Association* 105: 403-16.

————. 1981. *Plautus: Curculio*. Chico, Calif.

————. 1982. "Plautus," in *Ancient Writers: Greece and Rome*. New York, pp. 501-23.

Zagagi, Netta. 1980. *Tradition and Originality in Plautus*. Göttingen.

Zeitlin, Froma. 1982. "Travesties of Gender and Genre in Aristophanes' *Thesmophoriazusae*." *Reflections of Women in Antiquity*, pp. 169-217, ed. Helene Foley. London.

INDEX LOCORUM

INDEX NOMINUM ET RERUM

Page numbers in italics indicate a principal discussion or definition of that entry.